Library of
Davidson College

Ezra Pound at his daughter's home, Brunnenburg, in the Italian Tyrol, 1958.

EZRA POUND
perspectives

EZRA POUND
perspectives

essays in honor of his eightieth birthday

edited with an introduction by NOEL STOCK

GREENWOOD PRESS, PUBLISHERS
WESTPORT, CONNECTICUT

Library of Congress Cataloging in Publication Data

Stock, Noel, ed.
  Ezra Pound perspectives.

  Reprint of the ed. published by H. Regnery, Chicago.
  CONTENTS: Aiken, C. Ezra Pound, 1914.--Read, H.
Ezra Pound.--Moore M. Tribute.--Kenner, H. Leucothea's
bikini. [etc.]
  1. Pound, Ezra Loomis, 1885-1972--Addresses, essays,
lectures. I. Pound, Ezra Loomis, 1885-1972. II. Title.
[PS3531.082Z842 1976]   811'.5'2   75-40995
ISBN 0-8371-8712-5

811
P87xst1

Copyright © 1965 by Henry Regnery Company

Originally published in 1965 by Henry Regnery Company, Chicago

Reprinted with the permission of Henry Regnery Company

Reprinted in 1977 by Greenwood Press, Inc.

Library of Congress Catalog Card Number 75-40995

ISBN 0-8371-8712-5

Printed in the United States of America

79-4455

ACKNOWLEDGMENTS

I would like to thank Mrs. Dorothy Pound for her patience, assistance, and readiness to grant permission for the use of Ezra Pound copyright material. Also the poet's daughter, Mary de Rachewiltz, for giving up valuable time to locate papers in the Pound archive at Brunnenburg. I owe much also to Donald Gallup at Yale, Warren Roberts at Texas, and the following for permissions and assistance: Mrs. Ernest Hemingway, Mrs. Marion Cummings, Mrs. William Carlos Williams, Mrs. Anne Wyndham Lewis, Mrs. J. Biala (for permission to use the Ford Madox Ford letter), Miss Marianne Moore, Alister Kershaw (for permission to use the Richard Aldington letter), Captain Francis Newbolt, C.M.G. (for permission to use the Sir Henry Newbolt letter, © Francis Newbolt, 1965), the BBC, Yale University Library and the Library at the Humanities Research Center of the University of Texas. Copyright in the letter from T. S. Eliot belongs to Mrs. Eliot, to whom our thanks are due for permission to use it here. Thanks also for their help to Vanni Scheiwiller and Boris de Rachewiltz.

Sir Herbert Read's contribution is reprinted by permission of the American publisher, Horizon Press, of *The Tenth Muse* by Herbert Read, copyright 1957. Christine Brooke-Rose's essay is an expanded and revised version of one originally published in *A Review of English Literature*, Vol. II, No. 2, April, 1961, edited by A. N. Jeffares, University of Leeds, published by Longmans Green and Co., Ltd., London. A. Alvarez' essay "Ezra Pound" is reprinted with the permission of Charles Scribner's Sons from *Stewards of Excellence* by A. Alvarez, copyright © A. Alvarez, 1958. Allen Tate's contribution is from his *Collected Essays*, Allan Swallow, publisher, 1959. For permission to publish the letter by Rabindranath Tagore we thank Visva-Bharati, Calcutta. The Wyndham Lewis article is reprinted by permission of the *New Statesman*. I would like to thank Harcourt, Brace & World for permission to quote from *The Letters of Ezra Pound* and the Clarendon Press, Oxford, for permission to quote Nos. 38, 46 and 53 from R. A. B. Mynors' *Catullus* (Oxford Classical Texts). The translations from the Chinese in the BBC Third Program are reprinted by permission of the publishers from Ezra Pound's *The Classic Anthology Defined by Confucius*, Cambridge, Mass.; Harvard University Press, copyright 1954 by the President and Fellows of Harvard College. Thanks and acknowledgment are due also to *L'Herne* (Paris) for permission to use William Fleming's

"Ezra Pound and the French Language"; to the Society of Authors, London (who act for the James Joyce Estate), for permission to use the two James Joyce letters and for other valuable assistance; and to New Directions (and James Laughlin) for permission to use quotations from *Personae,* copyright 1926, 1954 by Ezra Pound; *The Literary Essays,* all rights reserved; *Section: Rock-Drill,* copyright © 1956 by Ezra Pound; and *The Cantos,* copyright 1934, 1937, 1940, 1948 by Ezra Pound. The Yeats letter is copyright © 1965 Miss Anne Yeats and Mr. Michael Butler Yeats, to whom our thanks are due; the poem "flotsam and jetsam" in Peter Whigham's essay is copyright 1940, by e.e. cummings, and is reprinted from his volume *Poems 1923–1924* by permission of Harcourt, Brace & World, Inc.

The cover photo was taken when e. e. cummings and his wife (Marion Morehouse) visited Pound in St. Elizabeth's Hospital, Washington, D.C., early in 1946.

INTRODUCTION

by Noel Stock

IT IS TYPICAL that when, through the good offices of Miss Kate Buss, the Authors' Club in the United States wanted to help T. S. Eliot in June, 1922, the bank draft for $200 should have been sent by way of Ezra Pound. As with so much else that was going on in the world of English letters at the time, he was somewhere to be found. Not necessarily as moving force, not always playing a leading part, but somewhere: putting in a good word for so-and-so here, writing to Yeats asking him to use his influence there, introducing this writer to that editor or recommending an indifferent poem on account of two excellent lines. He discovered Robert Frost and was one of the first to praise D. H. Lawrence, long before Lawrence was known. He was, at the same time, assisting Yeats toward a new astringency of style (in itself enough to give him a place in the history of English poetry), and ushering into print, against opposition, the work of Joyce and Eliot.

All this, while writing much of his own best work: verse, some of which may be counted in the small body of important poetry composed during the first half of the century, and prose undoubtedly among the most influential of the time. And even during the 1930's, when the political and economic aspects of his career came prominently into view and he often seemed to have lost touch with literature and the arts, he arranged a series of intensive musical concerts at Rapallo, which many have remembered with pleasure, and wrote a number of cantos widely praised for skill if not always for content. And he was still able to find time to write a charming letter to an English schoolboy giving him permission to reprint the poem "Game of Chess" in the *Ink Pot,* magazine of the chess club at the John Gulson School in the Borough of Coventry. We are engaged obviously with one of the figures of the century.

Ezra Pound was born on October 30, 1885, at Hailey, Idaho, son of a land office employee. The family returned east a year or so later, and his father afterward was appointed an assayer at the Philadelphia Mint. Pound spent most of his boyhood on the outskirts of Philadelphia and in New York. He received his Ph.B. at Hamilton College, New York State, and later his master's degree at the University of Pennsylvania, where in 1906 he was awarded the Harrison Fellowship in Romanics, which enabled him to make his first independent trip to Europe.

He took a teaching post at Wabash College, Crawfordsville, Indiana, when he returned to the United States in 1907, but early the following year he set sail again for Europe, this time for good. He carried with him the manuscript of poems—some of them dating back to Philadelphia, 1906—which were published in Venice in June, 1908, under the title *A Lume Spento*.

His literary life began in earnest when he arrived in London about three months later. During the next twelve or thirteen years he published some twenty-five books of verse and prose, wrote five hundred or more articles for magazines and newspapers in England and the U.S., married Dorothy Shakespear, launched a number of others upon their literary careers and guided Imagism, and helped to guide Vorticism, into literary history. No matter how strongly the poet himself has insisted upon the importance of other periods in his life, his own inner tendency has always been to remember the Venetian and London years with special affection. We have only to look at the Cantos, especially the Pisan sequence, to see this. And it is understandable that this should be so. For it is not in every decade that one gets into correspondence with an unknown impoverished Irish writer living on the Continent who has already written *Dubliners* and *Portrait of the Artist* and is about to embark on *Ulysses*. Nor every decade that one of the young Americans invited round for tea turns out to be T. S. Eliot.

Pound and Eliot first met on September 22, 1914; Eliot had recently been forced by the war to leave Marburg, Germany, where he was studying philosophy as a Harvard post-graduate student. In his first article on Eliot, a review of *Prufrock and Other Observations* for the *Egoist* of June, 1917, Pound wrote: "I have read the contents of this book over and over, and with continued joy in the freshness, the humanity, the deep quiet culture." Outlining the "New Poetry" for the *Future* a year later, he spoke of "a new French vitality among our younger writers of poetry," of whom Eliot "is the most finished, the most composed." He then quotes Eliot's "The Hippopotamus," which had appeared in the *Little Review* (of which Pound was the London editor!), and goes on:

> This cold sardonic statement is definitely of the school of Théophile Gautier; as definitely as Eliot's "Conversation Galante" is in the manner of Jules Laforgue. There is a great deal in the rest of Mr. Eliot's poetry which is personal, and in no wise derivative either from the French or from Webster and Tourneur; just as there is in "The Hippopotamus" a great deal which is not Théophile Gautier.

His happy knack of recognizing and saluting the best, almost at first sight, sometimes extended to the other arts. Thus in Wyndham Lewis' *Blast* (No. 1, June, 1914) he wrote: "Picasso and Kandinski, father and mother, classicism and romanticism of the movement." Although most of the works in which he was interested had not yet become public property, Pound himself was not one to restrict his message to a few fellow intellectuals. If the world would listen he was willing to preach. In 1918, for example, he wrote an article called "Henry James—The Last Phase" for the *Sunday Call* of Newark, New Jersey. It was the first of a series arranged by his father, but the rest were never published. It would be interesting now to know what cultural matter the *Sunday Call* found more important than a series of articles by Ezra Pound.

He left England in 1920 or '21 for Paris, where he wrote his opera, *Villon*. We find him reviewing Jean Cocteau's first book of poems and reading Proust:

> Proust's beautiful boredom rolls on, readable, very readable, and for once at least the precise nuance is recorded, and a future age will know what a dinner is like in the upper societies of the world, and will know as even the dear late H. J. never quite told them, the degree of vagueness of these people with regard to literature and the arts.
> ("Paris Letter," *Dial*, October, 1921)

And the following year, when *Ulysses* appeared, he published a long article called "James Joyce et Pécuchet" in the *Mercure de France*. He was also instrumental in publishing Hemingway's first book, *In Our Time* (Paris, 1924). Although *In Our Time* came out second, it was really, as the author explained in a letter to Dr. Gurney in 1924, the first in order of preparation for the press. It was number six in a series of small prose books edited by Pound for William Bird of the Three Mountains Press. Hemingway said that when it finally came out, *In Our Time* "was later than the three stories and ten poems," even though the manuscript had been in Bird's hands "long before" the other publisher, Robert McAlmon, had gone to work on his. In a letter to Pound dated July 22, 1933, Hemingway described himself as "friend and admirer." He had, he explained, received from Gertrude Stein some "damned good" advice, but much rubbish as well. *The Sun Also Rises* he had written in six weeks, starting it on his birthday, July 21, in Madrid, and finishing it on September 6 in Paris, without "sight nor sound" of her. It was, he said, from Pound that he had learned "more about how to write and how not to write" than from anyone else alive.

In 1924 Pound settled in Rapallo. The next twenty years, spent in Italy, coincided with his mounting interest in economics, politics and Confucius, which play an increasingly important part in the poetry he wrote during this time. He broadcast over Rome Radio while Italy and the U.S. were at war, and was arrested by the Americans in 1945 and charged with treason. The charge was never heard. He was sent to St. Elizabeth's Hospital, a government institution for the insane in Washington D.C., where for more than twelve years he read, wrote, received visitors and kept up a worldwide correspondence. When he was declared unfit to stand trial and the charge was dropped, on April 18, 1958, Pound returned to Italy, living first at his daughter's castle at Tirolo di Merano, in the Italian Tyrol, and moving later to Venice. He now spends most of the year in Venice, the summers in Rapallo.

Ezra Pound's sixty years of publishing activity—some 70 books of his own, contributions to 70 others and more than 1,500 articles—are expertly charted in Donald Gallup's *Bibliography of Ezra Pound* (London, 1963). Most of the writings upon which his fame now rests can be found in *Personae*, ("Collected Shorter Poems"), *The Cantos, The Spirit of Romance* and *The Literary Essays*.

CONTENTS

Introduction	vii	NOEL STOCK
Ezra Pound: 1914	2	CONRAD AIKEN
Ezra Pound	7	HERBERT READ
Tribute	21	MARIANNE MOORE
Leucothea's Bikini: Mimetic Homage	25	HUGH KENNER
Craft and Morals	41	A. ALVAREZ
Ezra Pound and Catullus	62	PETER WHIGHAM
The Search for Mrs. Wood's Program	78	DONALD GALLUP
Ezra Pound and the Bollingen Prize	86	ALLEN TATE
The Return of the Long Poem	90	HUGH MAC DIARMID
A Bundle of Letters	109	RABINDRANATH TAGORE
		T. S. ELIOT
		WYNDHAM LEWIS
		JAMES JOYCE
		MARIANNE MOORE
		HENRY NEWBOLT
		W. B. YEATS
		RICHARD ALDINGTON
		WILLIAM CARLOS WILLIAMS
		FORD MADOX FORD
		E. E. CUMMINGS
Ezra Pound and the French Language	129	WILLIAM FLEMING
A Note on Ezra Pound	151	ERNEST HEMINGWAY
Piers Plowman in the Modern Wasteland	154	CHRISTINE BROOKE-ROSE
The Fenollosa Papers	177	
An Appreciation	182	TOM SCOTT
The Rock Drill	198	WYNDHAM LEWIS
Ez Pound, Inc.	204	JOSEPH FETLER MALOF
BBC THIRD PROGRAM: Ezra Pound—Translations from the Chinese	210	DENIS GOACHER

ILLUSTRATIONS

Ezra Pound at his daughter's home, Brunnenburg, in the Italian Tyrol, 1958..*frontispiece*

"*How I Began*" *by Ezra Pound*........................... 1

"*Raphaelite Latin*," *written by Pound for the* Book News Monthly, *Philadelphia, September, 1906*................... 22

"*The Rune*" (*Gibraltar* [?], *March, 1908*), *page from Pound's 1908 notebook*, "*San Trovaso*."........................ 23

Galley proofs of The Spirit of Romance, *1910, corrected by the poet's father, Homer Pound*............................. 24

Cover of Mrs. Pound's copy of Provença, *1910, with the poet's autograph note about the color of the cover, an undistinguished tan* 31

"*Mistress Dorothy Shakespear*": *Pound's inscription to his future wife, in her copy of* Provença...................... 32

Title page of Provença.................................. 33

Dedication of Canzoni, *1911*............................ 67

First page of "*Redondillas*," *an unpublished poem of 114 lines deleted from* Canzoni. *The page proofs, now in the Humanities Research Center at the University of Texas, show that Pound first tried to revise the poem before deleting it altogether*........... 68

Mrs. Wood's program.................................. 79

Title page of T. S. Eliot's anonymous Ezra Pound: His Metric and Poetry, *1917*...................................... 97

Opening page of Ezra Pound: His Metric and Poetry....... 98

The first Pound bibliography, compiled by Pound himself for Eliot's Ezra Pound: His Metric and Poetry............99-101

James Joyce in Venice to Ezra Pound in London, 1915....112-13

Author's corrected typescript of Homage to Sextus Propertius, *1917*..137

The first separate edition of a Canto, distributed gratis, London, 1919..138

A notebook jotting by Pound, used in "*Canto VI*."..........139

Cover of Ernest Hemingway's In Our Time, *published in Paris, 1924, in a series edited by Pound*.........................152

Hemingway by Henry Strater for In Our Time. *Strater also designed the initials for Pound's* A Draft of XVI Cantos, *Paris, 1925*..152

Title page of In Our Time................................153

Opening page of In Our Time.............................153

In preparing his typescript for A Draft of XVI Cantos *(Paris, 1925), Pound made use of Cantos already published in Dial. These four introductory lines, added to pages of the Canto torn from the* Dial *of May, 1922, became "Canto II."*............164

"The Eighth Canto," from Dial, *as corrected to become part of "Canto II."*..165

Page-proof additions by the author, "Canto II," Paris edition of 1925...166

The poet with his father, Homer Pound, on Lake Garda, with Sirmione in the background..............................180

Pound with his granddaughter Patrizia and grandson Walter, at Brunnenburg, after his return to Italy, 1958..............181

Opening page of Pound's typescript of a small unpublished book, The Music of Beowulf, *circa late 1920's*...................187

A version of "Canto XLV," "With Usura," in the poet's own hand..188

Title page of Pound's Digest of the Analects, *Milan, 1937*...196

Colophon, Digest of the Analects...........................197

From Pound's corrected typescript of "Vou Club," an article on a group of Japanese poets. Although written for the Milwaukee Globe, *it was published in Ronald Duncan's* Townsman, *January, 1938*..202

Pound's corrected typescript of "Brace of Axioms" and opening of "Musik, as Mistaught," both published in the July, 1938, Townsman..203

Wrapper of Orientamenti, *Venice, 1944, one of the rarest of all Pound's books*..207

Pound's typescript of a section of the Pisan Cantos, *typed by the author at the U.S. detention camp at Pisa in 1945 and sent to his daughter, now Princess Mary de Rachewiltz*..........208

From Pound's corrected typescript of a two-page comment on Ezra Pound, *a book of essays edited by Peter Russell, 1950*....209

xiii

HOW I BEGAN.—BY EZRA POUND.

Poet and Critic: Author of "Personæ," "Canzoni," "Ripostes," &c.

If the verb is put in the past tense there is very little to be said about this matter.

The artist is always beginning. Any work of art which is not a beginning, an invention, a discovery, is of little worth. The very name Troubadour means a "finder," one who discovers. So far as the public is concerned my "career" has been of the simplest; during the first five years of it I had exactly one brief poem accepted by one American magazine, although I had during that time submitted "La Fraisne" and various other poems now held as a part of my best work. Net result of my activities in cash, five dollars which works out to about 4s. 3d. per year.

Mr. Elkin Mathews was the first publisher to whom I submitted my work in London. He printed my first three volumes, "Personae," "Exultations," and "Canzoni," at his own expense. So far as I can remember our only discussion of business was as follows :—

Mr. E. M. : "Ah, eh, do you care to contribute to the costs of publishing?"
Mr. E. P. : "I've got a shilling in my clothes, if that's any use to you."
Mr. E. M. : "Oh well, I rather want to publish 'em anyhow."

I have not yet received a brass farthing from these books, nor do I think that Mr. Mathews has up to date a clear balance against his expenses. One's name is known, in so far as it is known at all widely, through hearsay and reviews and through a wholesale quotation.

My books have made me friends. I came to London with £3 knowing no one.

I had been hungry all my life for "interesting people." I wanted to meet certain men whose work I admired. I have done this. I have had good talk in plenty.

I have paid a certain price, I have endured a certain amount of inconvenience, enough to put an edge on my enjoyment. I believe I have had more solid pleasure in life than any fellow of my years whom I have ever met.

I have "known many men's manners and seen many cities."

Besides knowing living artists I have come in touch with the tradition of the dead. I have had in this the same sort of pleasure that a schoolboy has in hearing of the star plays of former athletes. I have renewed my boyhood. I have repeated the sort of thrill that I used to have in hearing of the deeds of T. Truxton Hare; the sort that future Freshmen will have in hearing how "Mike" Bennet stopped Weeks. I have relished this or that about "old Browning, or Shelley sliding down his front banisters "with almost incredible rapidity."

There is more, however, in this sort of Apostolic Succession than a ludicrous anecdote, for people whose minds have been enriched by contact with men of genius retain the effects of it.

I have enjoyed meeting Victorians and Pre-Raphaelites and men of the nineties through their friends. I have seen Keats' proof sheets, I have had personal tradition of his time at second-hand. This, perhaps, means little to a Londoner, but it is good fun if you have grown up regarding such things as about as distant as Ghengis Khan or the days of Lope de Vega.

* * *

If by the question "How I began?" you mean "How did I learn my trade?" it is much too long to answer, and the details would be too technical.

I knew at fifteen pretty much what I wanted to do. I believed that the "Impulse" is with the gods; that technique is a man's own responsibility. A man either is or is not a great poet, that is not within his control, it is the lightning from heaven, the "fire of the gods," or whatever you choose to call it. His recording instrument is in his own charge. It is his own fault if he does not become a good artist—even a flawless artist.

I resolved that at thirty I would know more about poetry than any man living, that I would know the dynamic content from the shell, that I would know what was accounted poetry everywhere, what part of poetry was "indestructible," what part could *not be lost* by translation, and—scarcely less important—what effects were obtainable in *one* language only and were utterly incapable of being translated. In this search I learned more or less of nine foreign languages, I read Oriental stuff in translations, I fought every University regulation and every professor who tried to make me learn anything except this, or who bothered me with "requirements for degrees."

Of course, no amount of scholarship will help a man to write poetry, it may even be regarded as a great burden and hindrance; but it does help him to destroy a certain percentage of his failures. It keeps him discontented with mediocrity.

I have written a deal about technique for I detest a botch in a poem or in a donkey engine. I detest people who are content with botches. I detest a satisfaction with second-rateness.

As touching the Impulse, that is another affair. You may even call it "Inspiration." I do not mind the term, although it is in great disfavour with those who never experience the light of it.

The Impulse is a very different thing from the *furor scribendi*, which is a sort of emotional excitement due, I think, to weakness, and often preceding or accompanying early work. It means that the subject has you, not you the subject. There is no formula for the Impulse. Each poem must be a new and strange adventure if it is worth recording at all.

I know that for days the "Night Litany" seemed a thing so little my own that I could not bring myself to sign it. In the case of the "Goodly Fare" I was not excited until some hours after I had written it. I had been the evening before in the "Turkish Coffee" café in Soho. I had been made very angry by a certain sort of cheap irreverence which was new to me. I had lain awake most of the night. I got up rather late in the morning and started for the Museum with the first four lines in my head. I wrote the rest of the poem at a sitting, on the left side of the reading-room, with scarcely any erasures. I lunched at the Vienna Café, and later in the afternoon, being unable to study, I peddled the poem about Fleet Street, for I began to realise that for the first time in my life I had written something that "everyone could understand," and I wanted it to go to the people.

The poem was not accepted. I think the "Evening Standard" was the only office where it was even considered. Mr. Ford Madox Hueffer first printed the poem in his review some three months afterwards.

My other "vigorous" poem, the "Alta forte" was also written in the British Museum reading-room. I had had De Bom on my mind. I had found him untranslatable. Then it occurred to me that I might present him in this manner. I wanted the curious involution and recurrence of the Sestina. I knew more or less of the arrangement. I wrote the first strophe and then went to the Museum to make sure of the right order of permutations, for I was then living in Langham Street, next to the "pub," and had hardly any books with me. I did the rest of the poem at a sitting. Technically it is one of my best, though a poem on such a theme could never be very important.

I waited three years to find the words for "Piccadilly," it is eight lines long, and they tell me now it is "sentiment." For well over a year I have been trying to make a poem of a very beautiful thing that befell me in the Paris Underground. I got out of a train at, I think, La Concorde and in the jostle I saw a beautiful face, and then, turning suddenly, another and another, and then a beautiful child's face, and then another beautiful face. All that day I tried to find words for what this made me feel. That night as I went home along the rue Raynouard I was still trying. I could get nothing but spots of colour. I remember thinking that if I had been a painter I might have started a wholly new school of painting. I tried to write the poem weeks afterwards in Italy, but found it useless. Then only the other night, wondering how I should tell the adventure, it struck me that in Japan, where a work of art is not estimated by its acreage and where sixteen syllables are counted enough for a poem if you arrange and punctuate them properly, one might make a very little poem which would be translated about as follows :—

"The apparition of these faces in the crowd :
"Petals on a wet, black bough."

And there, or in some other very old, very quiet civilisation, some one else might understand the significance.

EZRA POUND: 1914

by Conrad Aiken

YES, THE YEAR is 1914, a half-century ago, and in Cambridge, Massachusetts, two young men were about to set sail for Europe, with a view to perhaps settling there. They were T. S. Eliot and myself. This was a subject we had many times discussed. Eliot, who had two years before returned from a year at the Sorbonne, sporting a cane and already a devotee of *Bubu de Montparnasse* and Laforgue and Vildrac, was in favor of trying France, but after a year of philosophizing in Germany first. But I, after several undergraduate visits to London and the Lake District and after spending part of a year there with my wife, so that I had some friends there, plumped for England. From an English girl who married one of the Dana family in Cambridge I had obtained letters of introduction to the then "new" English poets—Brooke, Davies, Flecker, Edward Thomas and Abercrombie—but most of all at that moment I was anxious to meet Ezra Pound, who seemed to me even then, apart from Eliot himself, the most exciting thing going. Eliot did not at this time share my enthusiasm for Pound.

I had some difficulty in finding anyone at Harvard who knew Pound, or even knew *of* him, but at last did so in the person of Hermann Hagedorn ("the good Hedgethorn" of one of Pound's earlier poems)—Harvard Class Poet of the year of 1907. I somehow dug up Hagedorn in Cambridge, extracted a note from him and, armed with my letters and with the typescript of "The Love Song of J. Alfred Prufrock," still unpublished and up to that point not even offered anywhere—for I don't think Eliot wholly shared my enthusiasm for it—I set off.

Well, of course we hadn't counted on the war, which was to change our plans entirely. It was Eliot, not myself, who was to settle in England, for he was caught behind the lines in Germany, and having managed after some delay to get himself circuitously to London, he very sensibly decided to stay there. As for me, the war greatly abbreviated my visit and the use to which I could put my letters of introduction, but in the six weeks or so allowed me I managed to meet all but Flecker— then dying in Switzerland—and Thomas, who couldn't come to London, but with whom I corresponded. Brooke and Davies were both more than kind to the young American poet— Brooke actually, in response to my note, came and knocked on my boardinghouse door in Bedford Place.

And Pound—? He too knocked on my boardinghouse door, but somewhat more loudly and challengingly. He hadn't cared much for Hagedorn, and for the sort of thing he wrote, as I didn't either, for that matter, and he not unnaturally viewed this newcomer with suspicion. But we got on very well in a guarded sort of way, and he was extremely kind in trying to introduce me to writers and publishers, although without much luck. I was to meet Hueffer—later Ford—and even to make up a foursome at tennis with him and Pound, but nothing came of this; perhaps the war intervened. And all that remains to me of that is Pound's constant repetition of Hueffer's slogan that poetry must be at least as well written as prose. We called on Yeats several times, always to find him out. A pity, too, for I never *did* meet either man. And similarly with the publishers. I was taken repeatedly to see John Lane, who in Pound's opinion was then the most "literate" of the publishers, but he too was never in. But it was typical of Pound's kindness, even to a potential enemy or rival, that he should have so persisted in trying to give me the right contacts.

Contacts: yes, these, as I was to discover, were of prime importance; they were part of the *game*. And for Pound it *was* a game, a super-chess game, and not without its Machiavellian elements. For example, this was the summer of the famous *Blast* dinner for the Vorticists, in which Wyndham Lewis was of course much involved. Pound sent me a card, which I still have, naming place and date, and saying, rather peremptorily, "I think you had better take this in." This put my back up. I had no intention then, or ever after, of joining any group or "movement," and I therefore sidestepped the Vorticists just as I sidestepped both the Imagists and the Amygists. I didn't attend the dinner, for which in a way I'm now sorry, and Pound never forgot or forgave. Nineteen years later, in an angry letter from Italy about some review I'd written which began: "Jeesus Gawd Aiken, you poor blithering ass," he concluded by saying: "I've never forgotten that you wouldn't go to the *Blast* dinner." I think it was in the same letter that he remarked something to the effect that when his history of the world came out I wouldn't have the sense to recognize it as such. The Cantos.

Meanwhile, however, we got on very well. I went many times to his queer triangular flat in Kensington, with its Gaudiers, and saw him, I suppose, on an average of about once a week. But the real clincher turned out to be "The Love Song of J. Alfred Prufrock." This I had shown to every conceivable editor in England, with no luck whatever. Harold Monro, at the Poetry Bookshop, which I had taken to frequenting and where Brooke had introduced me, at a "poetry squash," to Flint, Aldington, Hodgson and others, rejected Eliot's poem for *Poetry and Drama* as "crazy." He similarly dismissed "La Figlia Che Piange," which Eliot had sent me in a letter and which I showed to Monro at a party—I think he suspected it was a covert way of getting him to read a poem of my own. He was very rude about it, as only Monro could be, and as I was to remind him many years later, when we became very close friends and were together members of the *Criterion* circle.

And so, defeated everywhere by the English publishers, I naturally turned to Pound, who saw instantly that the poem was a work of genius, said that he would transmit it to Harriet Monroe for *Poetry*—no doubt *commanding* her to print it—and history was made.

This episode considerably increased Pound's respect for me, and led, in due course, to the meeting of Pound and Eliot, when Eliot made his escape from Germany. It led too to an impromptu lunch with Pound and Walter Lippmann at the Hotel Russell. I didn't know it, but it was the last time I was to see Pound in England—in fact, the next time I was to see him was in the Washington hospital, thirty-six years later. Wholly fortuitous: I climbed up to the top of a bus to find him there, and in a state of some agitation. He was to lunch with this Walter Lippmann, of a new paper called the *New Republic*, who was in England to look for a London correspondent for it. When I said that I knew Walter Lippmann very well—we had taken Copey's famous, or infamous, English 12 together—Pound begged me to come along as moral support. Not averse to a lunch at the expense of the *New Republic*, and glad of an opportunity to see Walter Lippmann again, I went along. It was a wonderful show. Pound was at his peacock best; he crackled with good talk and informed gossip while Lippmann, expressionless as a bronze Buddha, listened in respectful silence. It was a delicious lunch, too. And finally, after the coffee, and the paying of the quite formidable check, came the expected question. "Mr. Pound, can you suggest anyone here who would make a good London correspondent for us?" With no hesitation, Pound replied, "Why, I think *I* would!" Lippmann, not in the least dismayed, rose from his chair as if in dismissal, said, "Well, we can consider that," shook hands with us and departed. Needless to say, Pound didn't get the job; what was wanted was a political correspondent rather than a literary one, and an Englishman. But Pound had put on a brilliant performance, one that I never forgot.

After that, an increasing distance between us, both geographically and poetically, and very few letters. One, in the mid-twenties, said, "I gather from Eliot that you are not altogether wise in your choice of friends." There it was again—one had to stick to the Party Line. It was a warning to me that if I roved too far from the *Criterion* center I must face the consequences. Well meant, too, of course. But it is amusing as an example of the degree to which literary *politics* were then considered necessary, and indeed indispensable. I couldn't possibly go along with that. But just the same I feel and will always feel that I owe Pound an immense debt, not only for the great poetry and the many illuminations in his *obiter dicta,* but for his personal generosity. He was a good friend. And an admirable enemy!

EZRA POUND

by Herbert Read

The pages that follow were written several years ago, for an audience of young people unfamiliar with the name and significance of Ezra Pound. If I had to rewrite them I should make them more generous. I should say more about his poetry, and less about his poetics. On the poetry itself I agreed with Eliot: he was the most important living exemplar to the poets of our generation (I mean poets born between 1885 and the end of the century) and the development of a modern English poetry in our time would have been inconceivably different but for the intervention of his genius. It is not a question of counting the "gems" in his own verse, though they exist in plenty, but of acknowledging the skill of an alchemist who transmuted the debased counters of our language into pure poetic metal. "Remember this fire."

1965

I WILL BEGIN this tribute with some personal reminiscences, for they will show more clearly than my subsequent arguments why I approach the case of Ezra Pound in a sympathetic mood. Between 1912 and 1914 I was a student in a provincial university. I had just begun to write poetry and had been infected by that spirit of adventure or experiment that was about in those days. The fashionable poets were the Georgians—their annual anthology began to appear in the year 1913, and when the war broke out one of their number, Rupert Brooke, suddenly became a national poet, representative of much that was good in the spirit of the times, but also representative of something I had begun to recognize as sentimental and weak. My enlightenment was not due to native perspicacity so much as to the tutoring I had received from journals like the *New Age* and Wyndham Lewis' *Blast,* which journals carried on a rowdy opposition to all that the Georgians represented in literature and art.

By far the most active part in this opposition was played by a young American who had come to London in 1908 and had quickly made contact with the few figures in contemporary art and letters whom he could respect—W. B. Yeats, Wyndham Lewis, then just emerging as a self-styled Vorticist, and the belligerent philosopher T. E. Hulme. The intimate history of those prewar years has still to be written, but a group quite distinct from the Georgians began to form. Pound was joined by a young poet, Richard Aldington, along with his American wife, who signed her poems with the initials H. D.; by another American, John Gould Fletcher; and by a London poet, F. S. Flint.

In the spring or early summer of 1912, Pound, H. D. and Aldington decided that they were agreed upon certain principles of poetry, which they proceeded to formulate. In January of that year Hulme had collected in the *New Age* (January 25, 1912) five poems with the heading "The Complete Poetical Works of T. E. Hulme"—poems which were afterward reprinted as an appendix to one of Pound's volumes (*Ripostes,* October, 1912)—and it is certain that Hulme had a good deal to do with the clarification of the group's ideas. The group itself launched an anthology called *Des Imagistes,* which was edited by Pound and published in March, 1914. By the next year the group had split and a new anthology, *Some Imagist Poets,* was published, containing work by Aldington, H. D., Fletcher, Flint, D. H. Lawrence and Amy Lowell, but nothing by Pound.

Meanwhile the European war had broken out, and all these groups were forcibly dispersed. But the same event had dispersed the group of students to which I belonged, and for the first time—it was early in 1915—I went to London. There were, of course, many people whom I would have liked to meet at that time, but the poet with whom I most eagerly sought contact was Ezra Pound. I forget exactly when I first met Pound, but I had written to him and he immediately invited me to tea. He then lived in a triangular room in the Holland Park district of London. The person I met was probably as shy and embarrassed as I was, and I took away the impression of an agile lynx, beautiful in features, aggressively dressed, who sprang from conversational point to point very much in the manner that the animal he reminded me of might spring from branch to branch. We met occasionally in the ensuing years, but never became intimate; and then, shortly after the end of the war (I think it was in 1920), Pound left England in disgust and went to live at Rapallo, and from that time I saw less of him than ever. I met him for the last time the year before World War II, during a visit of his to London. I took away from that final meeting an impression of a man who had become agitated and elated to a dangerous degree.

There are, as everyone knows, degrees of mental disturbance, many of which do not merit incarceration. No unprejudiced observer will fail to observe in Pound's letters a progressive egocentricity, and even the cause of it is not far to seek. A man who sets out (1908) with the idea that "no art ever yet grew by looking into the eyes of the public" is bound to find himself increasingly isolated from the social matrix that ensures "sanity" (which admittedly may be no more than an accepted code of conduct). Pound started kicking against the pricks from the moment he landed in Europe, and the inertia of the brute that bore the pricks produced in him the frenzy of shrill vituperation, scatological abuse and mere spluttering invective which give his letters their wearisome unity. Of course one sympathizes, and sometimes the invective rises to a withering temperature. But then one remembers the inconsistency of it all. Pound professes a great admiration for Confucius; he translated the *Ta Hio* and other Confucian classics. But nothing could be further from the Confucian demeanor than Pound's roaring crusade. The Master said, "He who speaks without modesty will find it difficult to make his words good." That is only one of a hundred maxims from the *Analects* that might be brought to the attention of his self-styled disciple. The one virtue Confucius insisted on was "imperturbedness"; it is the one virtue that Pound has never possessed or professed. The fault lies in his displacement, his lack of "rootedness," his contempt for human failings. He lacks all humility—not so much personal humility, for he has never sought high rewards; but humility toward his art and toward his destiny. The distintegration which increasingly invades his poetry and his correspondence is simply a reflection of his failure to achieve any degree of social, and therefore personal, integration. "Galdós, Flaubert, Tourgenev, see them all in a death struggle with provincial stupidity. . . . All countries are equally damned, and all great art is born of the metropolis (or *in* the metropolis). The metropolis is that which accepts all gifts and all heights of excellence, usually the excellence that is *tabu* in its own village. The metropolis is always accused by the peasant of 'being made after foreign notions. '" There, in 1913 (and in spite of an admiration, expressed elsewhere, for such "peasant" poets as Homer and Hardy), is the Alexandrian heresy, of which Pound, in our time, has been the most gifted exponent.

What had drawn me to Pound, and made of me a devoted disciple, was his poetry and his poetics. But we both belonged to another and wider circle—that which centered around A. R. Orage, the editor of the *New Age,* one of the most influential personalities in the cultured life of that time. From Orage we had both acquired similar ideas about politics and economics, and though these were to lead us to very different conclusions, we always agreed on two points—the evil wrought in postmedieval society by the Church's admission of the principle of usury, and the dependence of any social revolution on its ability to deal with the monetary problem. There was another if a less urgent bond of interest: an enthusiasm for Chinese art and philosophy; but Pound was to develop this interest to a much deeper extent than I have done. On these three subjects—poetics, economics and sinology—Pound and I have always agreed, and this has perhaps enabled me to penetrate with more sympathy than would otherwise have been possible into the difficult problems raised by his work and conduct.

I shall concentrate mainly on Pound's poetry and poetic principles, but his poetry is so involved with his ideas that some appreciation of these is also essential. Pound would maintain, and I think I would agree with him, that there is an intimate connection between the general decline of sensibility which has led to the most vulgar civilization in the history of mankind and the economic fallacies which began with the religious and legal recognition of usury at the end of the Middle Ages. In other words, poetics and economics cannot be separated. But for the moment let us turn our attention to the poetics.

So far as the English-speaking world is concerned, Pound is the animator if not the founder of the modern movement in poetry. His experiments—with the exception of the five or six poems which T. E. Hulme wrote in 1908[1]—predate any similar experiments by other English or American poets. By this I do not mean that there was no free verse before 1912. Pound did not invent free verse; he reformed free verse, gave it a musical structure, and to that extent we may say paradoxically that it was no longer free. But let us try to trace the historical process in Pound's own work. As a youth he must have modeled himself on romantic poets like Chatterton and Poe, on Rossetti and Swinburne. Then he discovered Italian poetry, possibly via Rossetti, and then the Troubadours and Browning. The result was an eclectic style to which, as time went on, were added accents from Lionel Johnson and Dowson, W. B. Yeats and Fiona Macleod. These *pastiches* are not to be despised; a poem like "The Goodly Fere" has found its way into many anthologies, and it is indeed a good fake of a medieval ballad. Most of the verse included in the first three volumes Pound published in England between 1909 and 1911 is of this nature—romantic poetry in the true historical meaning of that ambiguous word. Several of these poems are accompanied by learned footnotes—Mr. Eliot was not the first poet to indulge in this practice. A footnote to "La Fraisne," for example, refers the reader to

[1] I have given the evidence for Hulme's priority in *The True Voice of Feeling*, chap. vi.

Janus of Basel, the "Daemonalitas" of Father Sinistrari of Ameno (*circa* 1600), the Book of the Dead and the Provençal sources of the legend on which the poem is based.

Such was the stage of development Pound had reached by 1911 or 1912, when he began his discussions with Hulme, Aldington and Flint. What then emerged was "The School of Images," or Imagism, as it was to be called. Like the sonneteering of the sixteenth century, it was of foreign inspiration, mainly French, though we must not forget Walt Whitman, who at any rate served as a terrible warning. Later Pound was to make "A Pact" with him:

> I make a pact with you, Walt Whitman—
> I have detested you long enough.
> I come to you as a grown child
> Who has had a pig-headed father;
> I am old enough now to make friends.
> It was you that broke the new wood,
> Now it is a time for carving.
> We have one sap and one root—
> Let there be commerce between us.

But for the moment it was "a time for carving," and it was the French poets, Gautier and the later Symbolists, Verlaine, Francis Jammes, Paul Fort, Tristan Corbière, Max Elskamp, Mallarmé, Maeterlinck and Verhaeren and, of course, Rimbaud, who were the master carvers. But in France itself a new group of *vers libristes* had come into existence, and with this group—Jules Romains, André Spire, Vildrac and Duhamel—the English group soon established a sympathetic exchange of ideas. The guiding critic was Remy de Gourmont, whose *Livre des Masques* had given definition to the whole movement, and whose *Problème du Style* is a source book for many of the ideas that inspired the literary developments in both France and England at this time. I am afraid it has been forgotten how much we all owed to this brilliant critic. Pound was in direct communication with him until his death.

When, as a result of all this cross-fertilization of ideas, the group in England began to formulate their principles, they took the following shape: I give them in Pound's own words:

In the spring or early summer of 1912, "H.D.", Richard Aldington and myself decided that we were agreed upon the three principles following:
1. Direct treatment of the "thing" whether subjective or objective.
2. To use absolutely no word that does not contribute to the presentation.
3. As regarding rhythm: to compose in the sequence of the musical phrase, not in sequence of a metronome.

And here are some further injunctions which Pound wrote in a poetry magazine in 1913:

Use no superfluous word, no adjective, which does not reveal something.

Don't use such an expression as "dim lands of peace". It dulls the image. It mixes an abstraction with the concrete. It comes from the writer's not realizing that the natural object is always the *adequate* symbol.

Go in fear of abstractions (Remy de Gourmont had said: *"En littérature, comme en tout, il faut que cesse le règne des mots abstraits"*—this was on the 27th February, 1898—Preface to *Le deuxième livre des masques*).

Do not re-tell in mediocre verse what has already been done in good prose.

Don't imagine that the art of poetry is any simpler than the art of music, or that you can please the expert before you have spent at least as much effort on the art of verse as the average piano teacher spends on the art of music.

Use either no ornament or good ornament.

And so on, to advice of a more technical nature.

The Imagist anthology of 1915 (in which Pound did not appear) had a more elaborate statement of principles, but they are mostly covered by Pound's statement. One paragraph in this manifesto gives a clear definition of the word Imagist and may therefore be usefully quoted:

To present an image. We are not a school of painters, but we believe that poetry should render particulars exactly and not deal in vague generalities, however magnificent and sonorous. It is for this reason that we oppose the cosmic poet, who seems to us to shirk the real difficulties of his art.

We might explain Pound's later development by saying that he began with free verse of a vaguely rhetorical kind, and arrived at a specific kind of free verse to which he gave the name "Imagism." Imagism differs from Whitmanesque and other varieties of free verse in insisting on a concreteness of imagery, and on a tight musical or rhythmical structure. Nothing is in a certain sense less free than good free verse, for it achieves an exact correspondence between the verbal and rhythmical structure of the verse and the mood or emotion to be expressed. The result is a quality which Mr. Eliot has recently called "transparent"—"that is to say, you listen not to poetry as poetry, but to the meaning of poetry." In Pound's words, you get rid of the ornament. And when you are rid of the ornament you are left with the image, the direct percept. The trouble in our kind of language is that we have to express ourselves in words which do not visually convey the image. It is different in the Chinese language, where the ideogram is developed from a visual representation of the image, and where, however remotely, a suggestion of the concrete object is present in the verbal sign.

I must now deal briefly with Pound's theory of poetry as it developed beyond Imagism. This is based almost entirely on one short treatise, "The Chinese Written Character As a Medium for Poetry," by Ernest Fenollosa. Fenollosa was an American orientalist who died in 1908. I have never known whether Pound had direct contact with this distinguished scholar, but it was Pound who first published this particular essay in 1918. It is undoubtedly one of the basic documents of the aesthetics of modern art, and provides the bridge between the oriental and occidental cultures.

Fenollosa begins with an analysis of the Chinese sentence, and more particularly of that sentence when it constitutes a poem. I cannot enter into the details of Fenollosa's argument, but he brings out the essential concreteness of the language, a concreteness that extends to verbs, conjunctions and pronouns as well as to ordinary nouns. More significantly still, he shows how the Chinese have built up their intellectual fabric, their logical categories, in the same concrete way. They have done this by the use of metaphor, that is to say, the use of material images to suggest immaterial relations. The rest of the argument can be given in Fenollosa's own words:

> The whole delicate substance of speech is built upon substrata of metaphor. Abstract terms, pressed by etymology, reveal their ancient roots still embedded in direct action. But the primitive metaphors do not spring from arbitrary *subjective* processes. They are possible because they follow objective lines of relations in nature herself.
>
> Metaphor, the revealer of nature, is the very substance of poetry. The known interprets the obscure, the universe is alive with myth. The beauty and freedom of the observed world furnish a model, and life is pregnant with art. It is a mistake to suppose, with some philosophers of aesthetics, that art and poetry aim to deal with the general and the abstract. This conception has been foisted upon us by medieval logic. Art and poetry deal with the concrete in nature . . . . Poetry is finer than prose because it gives us more concrete truth in the same compass of words.
>
> Our ancestors built the accumulations of metaphor into structures of language and into systems of thought. Languages today are thin and cold because we think less and less into them.
>
> In diction and in grammatical form science is utterly opposed to logic. Primitive men who created language agreed with science and not with logic. Logic has abused the language which they left to her mercy.
>
> Poetry agrees with science and not with logic.
>
> The moment we use the copula, the moment we express subjective inclusions, poetry evaporates . . . . We need in poetry thousands of active words, each doing its utmost to show forth the motive and vital forces . . . .
>
> We should beware of English grammar, its hard parts of speech, and its lazy satisfaction with nouns and adjectives. We should seek and at least bear in mind the verbal undertone of each noun. We should avoid "is" and bring in a wealth of neglected English verbs.
>
> . . . The great strength of our language lies in its splendid array of transitive verbs. . . . These give us the most individual characterizations of force. Their power lies in their recognition of nature as a vast storehouse of

forces. . . . Will is the foundation of our speech. . . . I had to discover myself why Shakespeare's English was immeasurably so superior to all others. I found that it was his persistent, natural, and magnificent use of hundreds of transitive verbs. . . . A study of Shakespeare's verbs should underlie all exercises in style.

In this last passage we have indicated the clue to the technique of Pound's later verse—the verse of the Cantos. It achieves its poetic effect by the *juxtaposition* of words whose *overtones* blend into a delicate and lucid harmony. A shorter definition still: Poetry is the placing of words to produce metaphorical overtones. "The overtones vibrate against the eye." Shorter still, a definition suggested to Pound by a Japanese student: "Poetry consists of gists and piths."

Pound's literary criticism is developed in several volumes, beginning with *The Spirit of Romance* (1910), *Instigations* (1920), *Indiscretions* (1923), "How to Read" (1931), *The ABC of Reading* (1934), *Polite Essays* (1937), *Guide to Kulchur* (1938); but the cream of it all is contained in the volume of collected essays called *Make It New,* published in 1934. Here are Pound's articles on the Troubadours, on the Elizabethan Classicists, the translators of Greek, on French poets, on Henry James and Remy de Gourmont, and on Cavalcanti, the late thirteenth-century Italian poet to whom Pound has devoted so much attention.

Criticism, according to Pound, has two functions. First, it is a rationale of composition—it tries "to fore-run composition, to serve as gun-sight." Secondly, it is a process of "excernment." "The general ordering and weeding out of what has actually been performed. The elimination of repetitions. The work analogous to that which a good hanging committee or a curator would perform in a National Gallery or in a biological museum." Even this second function is for the benefit of the actual composer, for it is further defined as "the ordering of knowledge so that the next man (or generation) can most readily find the live part of it, and waste the least possible time among obsolete tissues."

It will be seen at once that this very drastically limits the scope of criticism. That scope, as defined by representative critics such as Coleridge, Matthew Arnold and T. S. Eliot, has included not merely the composer but also the audience. Admittedly much criticism suffers from not clearly separating these two points of view, and most of our critics make for confusion by continually jumping without warning from one point of view to the other. Pound avoids that danger. His intention is always clear, his judgment unequivocal. Not the shade of an ethical prejudice discolors his purely literary opinions. We may say that he has one general principle of criticism, and one only: "Civilization is individual." That principle is often reiterated throughout his work, and underlies his poetics, his ethics and even his economics. As to what Mr. Pound believes—his answer to Mr. Eliot's worried question was: "I believe in the *Ta Hio*." That is not a witticism: Pound has studied Confucius and devoted a great deal of time to the translation and elucidation of the Confucian texts. There is one famous saying of the Chinese sage which perfectly expresses the general character of Pound's criticism: "What the superior man seeks is in himself; what the small man seeks is in others." Pound, as we have seen, is in some sense a traditionalist: he has studied the past; but in the end he relies on his individual sensibility. Literature, he would say, depends for its cultivation and continuance on the peculiar sensibility of a few artists within each generation. Criticism is a professional activity—a process of refinement, above all, a refinement of language to make it new, to make it precise, to make it clear.

There is plenty of evidence to show that he has applied his critical faculties to his own work, and there is no modern poet whose work shows such a decisive development from birth to maturity. I shall not try to illustrate this development; it would require too much quotation. Any educated reader who knows an early romantic poem such as "La Fraisne," a perfect free-verse cadence such as "Doria," one of the "translations" from the Chinese such as "The River-Merchant's Wife" and the *Hugh Selwyn Mauberley* sequence (the most "carved" satirical verse in the language) will be incited, if liable to the poetic contagion, to fill in the evolutionary gaps.

By 1920, when *Mauberley* was published, Pound was already engaged in the immense work which was to occupy him for the rest of his life, and which is still unfinished. It has never been given a definite title, but is known as the Cantos; more than ninety of these have already been published.[2] They are of varying length, but they already amount to more than five hundred pages of verse and constitute the longest, and without hesitation I would say the greatest, poetic achievement of our time.

Technically the poem is the perfection of Pound's taut free verse, and there are passages of the purest lyricism which, in themselves, if extracted, would constitute a body of poetry for which there is no contemporary parallel. In the complex structure of the Cantos these passages are relatively rare, and what we have to explain is a mosaic of images, ideas, phrases—politics, ethics, economics—anecdotes, insults, denunciations—English, Greek, Latin, Italian, Provençal, Chinese —without division, without transition, without cohesion, apparently without structure and without pattern. But all the same there *is* pattern, there *is* structure and there is a controlling force. Pound himself has used the image of the magnet and the iron filings: "The *forma,* the immortal *concetto,* the concept, the dynamic form which is like the rose-pattern driven into the dead iron filings by the magnet, not by material contact with the magnet itself, but separate from the magnet itself. Cut off by a layer of glass, the dust and filings rise and spring into order. Thus the *forma,* the concept rises from death."

The dust and filings: these are the detritus of a civilization in decay, in dissolution. The Cantos must be conceived as a massive attack on this civilization, an exposure of its rottenness and active corruption. It is an analysis of history—of European and American history since the Middle Ages, and of the grandiose epochs of Chinese history. Corruption is traced to its source in usury, and those who have opposed usury and tried to eradicate it—Malatesta and Jefferson, for example—

---

[2] The total is now 109, with parts of a few additional Cantos published in magazines.—*Ed.*

are treated as heroes in this epic. Against this corruption is set the harmony and ethical rectitude of Confucius.

I am not going to deny that for the most part the Cantos present insuperable difficulties to the impatient reader but, as Pound says somewhere, "you can't get through hell in a hurry." I am not going to defend the poem in detail; there are stretches which I find boring, but that too is no doubt a characteristic of hell. But I am convinced of the greatness of the poem as a whole, and the more I read it the more I get out of it. It will need in the future an immense work of exegesis, and in America that work has already begun. In the end the poem cannot fail to have its effect. In his criticism Pound frequently uses the phrase "ideas in action," and that is the general characteristic of the texture of this immense poem. Ideas do not exist as abstract counters in a process of logical reasoning; rather, they are dropped into the mind of the reader as separate concrete entities which then set up mental reactions. Conceptual reasoning is not the poet's business; it is his business to see, to present, to condense, to combine—all active processes. Pound's favorite Chinese ideograph represents man and word side by side: a man standing by his word, a man of his word, truth.

If I do not discuss these ideas on the present occasion, it is not because I consider them nonsense. On the contrary, I think that Pound is one of the few men who have talked sense in our time. The mistake he has made, in my opinion, is to believe that his ideas could be realized by a modern state. He did not see that the modern totalitarian state is an incarnation of the principle of usury, an instrument of war and oppression. Because Mussolini was fighting the international bankers, Pound thought that he had turned his back on the monetary game, had seen through "the great illusionistic monetary monopoly." But he was wrong—tragically blind and wrong—and he paid the penalty exacted by a revengeful victor. Pound has always hated war; he did not think that youth and beauty should be sacrificed

> For an old bitch gone in the teeth,
> For a botched civilization.

His broadcasts from Italy during the last war were legal acts of treason against the United States. But Pound would never admit that the United States, in any human sense, was committed to the war: the United States was involved in a disaster precipitated by Wall Street. Usury is a cancer, Finance a disease and War the dying agony of a civilization strangled by debt and taxation. These were the ideas that Pound attempted to put into action during the war. Twenty years have passed since the end of the war, debts have mounted, taxation has increased, the economic chaos is worse than ever and the threat of war is always with us. In the circumstances, who can say that Pound was wrong? His ideas are still in action.

TRIBUTE

by Marianne Moore

WHAT Ezra Pound required of poetry, he exemplified in person, I think: [Cicero] Ut doceat, ut moveat, ut delectet: teach, stir the mind, afford enjoyment—his three offices of the orator.

"Raphaelite Latin," written by Pound for the Book News Monthly, *Philadelphia, September, 1906.*

Raphaelite Latin

By Ezra Pound

[Mr. Pound, who is Fellow in Romance languages for the University of Pennsylvania, and is especially interested in late Latin, has spent the past summer traveling in Europe, gathering material by the way. He is ready to defend the Latin of this period—which has the lifetime of Raphael as its center—from the superficial charges of literary barrenness and inferiority of production that have been made against it. Some idea of the mere bulk of this production may be gained from the fact that the Ghero collection alone, if complete, would contain nearly three thousand pages of Latin verse.—THE EDITORS.]

PERHAPS the most neglected field in all literature is that containing the Latin works of the elegant poets and scholars contemporary with Raphael, and owning for the most part Pietro Bembo as their chief.

There are causes for this neglect. The scholars of classic Latin, bound to the Germanic ideal of scholarship, are no longer able as of old to fill themselves with the beauty of the classics, and by the very force of that beauty inspire their students to read Latin widely and for pleasure; nor are they able to make students see clearly whereof classic beauty consists. The scholar is compelled to spend most of his time learning what his author wore and ate, and in endless pondering over some utterly unanswerable question of textual criticism, such as: "In a certain epigram," not worth reading, and which could not get into print to-day, "is a certain word *seca* or *secat?* The meaning will be the same, but the syntax different." The scholar is bowed down to this Germanic ideal of scholarship, the life work of whose servants consists in gathering blocks to build a pyramid that will be of no especial use except as a monument, and whose greatest reward is the possibility that the servant may have his name inscribed on the under side of some half-prominent stone, where by a chance—a slender one—some future stone-gatherer will find it. This system has these results; it makes the servant piously thank his gods that his period ends A. D. 400, and that there are some stones he need not carry, some things written thereafter that he need not read. It also prevents his building a comfortable house for his brain to live in, and makes him revile anyone who tries so to do with the object and utterly scornful "dilettante." No one knows the contempt and hatred that can be gathered into these few syllables until they have been hissed at him by one truly Germanized.

The scholars of Romance languages pass over these Latin poems as not strictly belonging to any of the Romance literatures—French, Italian, or Spanish. And the students of Renaissance history are too much occupied with the greater names of the period in politics, painting, and sculpture to turn their attention to lesser men of letters.

Bembo's name has, of course, come down to us; Castiglione stands because of his works in a newer tongue; and of the odd hundred other poets of the early Renaissance some few names remain known to us by virtue of their deeds in other fields, or in connection with the resplendent family of the Medici, and as satellites of its flower, Lorenzo the Magnificent. Lorenzo was born in 1449, and Bembo died in 1547.

In this time also had flourished that wonderful friendship between Michael Angelo and Vittoria Colonna, which proved once and for all that genius has no age, and made the man of more than three-score write sonnets, and draw with all his youth's first vigor.

True, much of the Latin verse of this period is filled with greetings, high-sounding greetings in the market-place from one scholar to another, as compliment for his new edition of some re-edited or rediscovered classic; or to some hoped-for patron, as compliment for nothing whatever.

Literature stood thus: Petrarch had based his fame on his Latin epic the "Africa;" Dante alone had dared to put a master poem in the speech of the people; Latin was still the language of the schools, and good Latin it was, too. All

"The Rune" (Gibraltar [?], March, 1908), page from Pound's
1908 notebook, "San Trovaso."

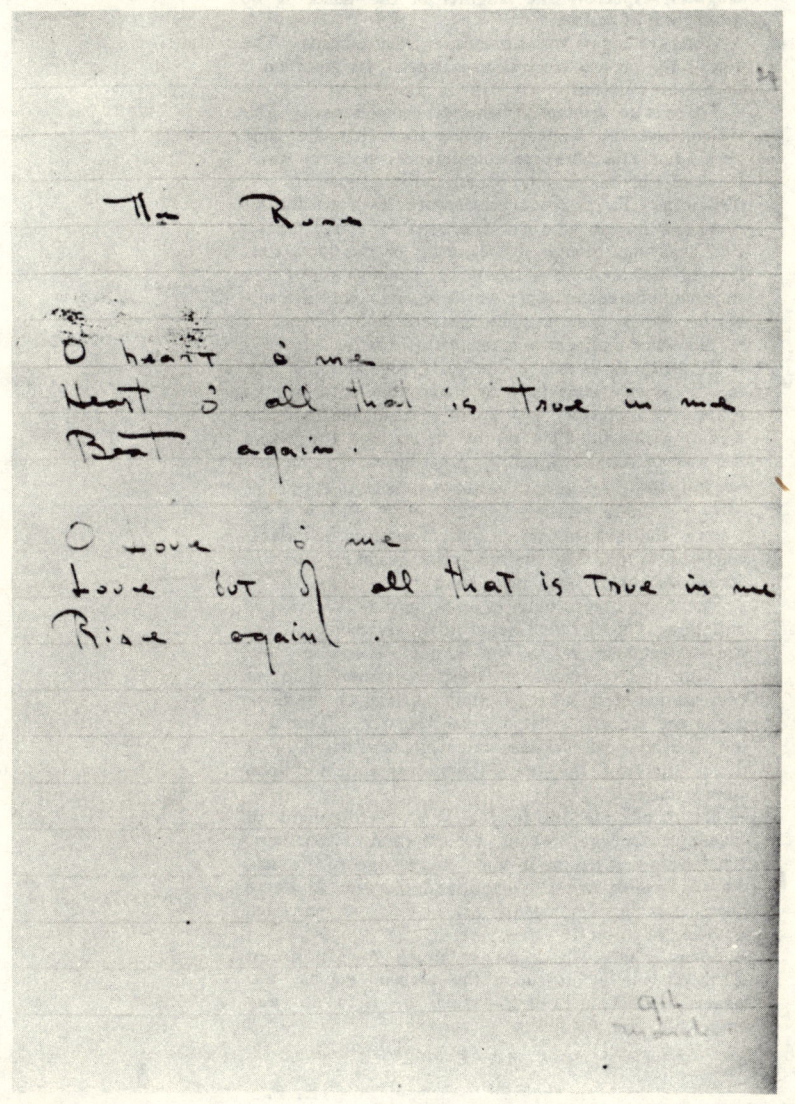

Galley proofs of The Spirit of Romance, *1910, corrected by the poet's father, Homer Pound.*

laughter, especially the laughter of the mind, is no mean form of ecstasy.

Good art begins with an escape from dullness. The aim of the present work is to instruct. Its ambition is to instruct painlessly.

There is no attempt at historical completeness. The "Grundriss von Grüber" covers somewhat the same period and falls short of completeness in divers ways. It consists of 21,000 folio pages, and is, needless to say, Tedescan. To this admirable work I cheerfully recommend anyone who has a passion for completeness. For, omitting, though it does, many of the facts concerning mediæval literature, it yet contains references to some hundreds of other works wherein the curiosity of the earnest may in some measure be staked; as to my fitness or unfitness to attempt this treatise.

Putnam tells us that, in the early regulations of the faculty of the University of Paris, this oath is prescribed for professors: "I swear to read and to finish reading within the time set by the statutes, the books and parts of books assigned for my lectures."[1] This law

[1] This meant from four to six books for the Doctors of Law or Medicine. Usually one professor had one book on which to lecture.

I have, contrary to the custom of literary historians, complied with. My multitudinous mistakes and inaccuracies are at least my own.

The book treats only of such mediæval works as still possess an interest other than archæological for the contemporary reader who is not a specialist. My criticism has consisted in selection rather than in presentation of opinion. Certain portions of the book are in the strictest sense original research. Throughout the book all critical statements are based on a direct study of the texts themselves and not upon commentaries.

My thanks are due to Mr Wm. P. Shepherd of Hamilton College, whose refined and sympathetic scholarship first led me to some knowledge of French, Italian, Spanish and Provençal, and likewise to Padre Jose Maria de Eligondo, for his kindness to me when studying in Spain.

Some stigma will doubtless attach to Mr Ernest Rhys, at whose instigation the present volume was undertaken. Guilty of collusion, he is in no way responsible for its faults.

Amplissimas ac manu qui transcripsit gratias.

E. P.

LEUCOTHEA'S BIKINI: MIMETIC HOMAGE

by Hugh Kenner

POUND'S CHARACTERISTIC ACT—the running paraphrase, the torqued translation, the quick skim of his light across glints hidden to any blander gaze at alien surfaces—goes unnoticed by the terminology he has himself furnished to criticism, and so gets dismissed as idiosyncrasy, intruding into occasions for pure contemplation. The man who rendered an ideogram as "bigosh" seems not to be following the ideogrammic method, which entails (does it not?) a selfless interaction of nodal things, quirkiness subsumed in oriental calm. For ideograms, images, the right hand on the chisel, these belong to a poetic of objects; we assume perhaps too readily that a poem is like a statue, too tardily that it is like a drama, a drama enacted in time, before our minds, by the single actor, its maker.

"Imitation, then, being natural to us," wrote Aristotle, "as also the sense of harmony and rhythm, the meters being obviously species of rhythms, it was through their original aptitude, and by a series of improvements for the most part gradual on their first efforts, that they created poetry out of their improvisation." To see in a poem a poetic act is to see gestures of a performer, not incongruities in a statue. Consider Leucothea's bikini.

>   That the wave crashed, whirling the raft, then
>   Tearing the oar from his hand,
>   broke mast and yard-arm
>   And he was drawn down under the wave,
>   The wind tossing,
>   Notus, Boreas,
>   as it were thistle-down.
>   Then Leucothea had pity,
>   "mortal once
>   Who now is a sea-god:
>   *nostou*
>   *gaies Phaiēkōn,* . . ."[1]

So closes "Canto XCV," each phrase excerpted in sequence from the fifth book of the *Odyssey,* lines 313-45. The typography not only guides the voice, but manages to suggest that the Homeric page has been ventilated by simply underlining phrases. The last three words draw us down into the Greek itself, and the next Canto (the first in *Thrones*) opens with another Greek word, Leucothea's next contribution, before rising back into English as she slips into the water:

>   *Krēdemnon* . . .
>   *krēdemnon* . . .
>   and the wave concealed her,
>   dark mass of great water.

This is the black wave, *melan kyma,* into which she disappears at line 353; with her disappearance Pound's dealings with the episode cease. The one obscurity in this brilliantly selective paraphrase is *krēdemnon,* for which there happens not to be a simple English equivalent. Pound offered his gloss a page earlier:

>   "My bikini is worth yr/ raft". Said Leucothoe

She said something to this effect when she gave Odysseus her *krēdemnon,* the word Pound writes twice because it occurs

---

[1] I am transliterating all Greek, for the reader's comfort and the printer's.

twice in the Greek, when she offers it (346) and when she hands it over (351). Can it really be an Argive bikini? It is the magic garment that he is to spread under his chest till he gets to land, *"phylaktērion thatlattiou kakou,* a protector against evil seas," writes one scholiast, and *"hōsper symbalon tēs theias boētheias,* as a token of divine assistance," writes another, pointlessly explicit. Liddell and Scott are more helpful: "It seems to have been a sort of *veil* or *mantilla with lappets,* passing over the head and hanging down on each side, so that at pleasure it might be drawn over the face." Andromache, Juno and Penelope all wear one, so it is "mostly therefore worn by persons of rank," though in *Odyssey* vi, 100 Nausikaa's waiting-women toss off their *krēdemna* before playing ball. Whether or not it generally connotes rank, there is not doubt that it is a covering for the head; indeed, the word is metaphorically applied to "the battlements which top and crown a city's walls," and in both the *Iliad* and the *Odyssey* we find *Troiēs hiera krēdemna,* the sacred battlements of Troy. Though it isn't Homer's usual word for battlements, this metaphor can eliminate any lingering doubt that *krēdemnon* is associated with the head; and the trouble Pound has taken to write out the Greek word twice, at a point of maximum emphasis, suggests that he would have glanced at what Liddell and Scott have to say about it.

So why did the *krēdemnon* become a bikini? For several reasons; the first is the need for some remotely plausible equivalent for a word on which Liddell and Scott expended a paragraph. With tiller and yardarm gone, the raft a shuttlecock for wind gods, Poseidon Earthshaker rearing up great black waves, are we to pause for an archaeological footnote about the costumes of Greek ladies? Or to wonder why a sea nymph's costume includes something to put on her head? Something, moreover, with strings to tie it shut across her face? A miraculous garment is what the story requires, a miraculous garment wearable at sea.

This kind of difficulty has on other occasions pressed Pound to some of his most characteristic ingenuities. In "The Seafarer," for instance, we read

                    Dagas sind gewitene
        ealle onmedlan   eorthan rices

—days are departed, all the glory of earthly realms. Here Pound, having written "Days little durable," was brought up short, we may suppose, by the problem of an equivalent for *rices;* for though the "Seafarer" sensibility remains imbedded in the ninth century, words like *realms* and *kingdoms* have gone on acquiring sophisticated connotations. The king or Caesar of "The Seafarer" ("nearon nu cyningas ne caseras / ne goldgiefan. . .") is no more than the gold-giver, the personal overlord, at most the tribal head. A *kingdom,* on the other hand, is a political organization of some complexity, and *realm* is touched with the sumptuousness of *royaume.* In this difficulty the mere look of *rices* seems to have suggested a usable noun; whereupon the need for assonance supplied a stand-in for *onmedlan,* and *eorthan,* as though in response to the tug of the Anglo-Saxon words, became not earthly but earthen:

>And all arrogance of earthen riches.

Riches for *rices,* like some of the details in *Sextus Propertius,* has ever since suggested to suspicious minds a mistranslation; but no one has suggested anything better. It remains a plausible word in the modern poem, and a modern poem is what is being generated.

For Pound (this brings us to the second principle) exacts of his words that they sit easily on modern tongues, and moreover that we shall be aware of this fact. "The Seafarer" ensures our awareness by its very existence as a *tour de force;* only detailed comparison with the original will uncover the instances when the "correct" word has been replaced by the word that fits today. Elsewhere he is determined to hold before our minds a fact easily forgotten: that if, as Wyndham Lewis once put it, whole landslides from other times and tongues are coming onto his pages, it is into the twentieth century that they are sliding, at the bidding of a twentieth-century poet. The bikini of Leucothea, like the Frigidaire he imagined Sextus Propertius disclaiming, is precisely the contemporary note, both the shock of a reality beyond normal imaginative reality, and the stubborn reminder that transposition, not recreation, is going on, that the mind remains anchored in these times, not those.

For he is not an illusionist: his aesthetic is older, more catholic, than Ibsen's. As Shakespeare, suspending the miracle, bids us remember that before our eyes on the stage "some squeaking Cleopatra," a boy-Cleopatra, is miming "the posture of a whore," so Pound does not offer the flawless miraculous product but dramatizes an imaginative process.

The process is easily seen in the China Cantos, where we find, superimposed, three things: (1) a bare high chronicle manner moving to the clash of oriental cymbals and drums, paraphrase of some dynastic record that does not exist, being generated in (2) the imagination of an American who is (3) exiled in twentieth-century Italy and leafing through a multi-volumed history[2] published in eighteenth-century France. In "Canto LVI" all these elements are readily separable.

> Slept on the pine needle carpet
> > sprinkled horse blood
> praying no brave man be born among Mongols

—that is the chronicle.
> Billets, biglietti, as coin was too heavy for transport
> > but redeemed the stuff at one third
>
> And Ou-Kiai had another swat at the tartars
> > and licked 'em

—that is the American paraphraser, in Italy.
> ⁻ HONG VOU voyant ses forces affoiblir
> > dict: Que la vertu t'inspire, Tchu-ouen.

—that is his French book.

The whole being meant to wear this look of rapid resourceful paraphrase, Pound followed the appropriate method, which was to work through the French volumes setting down rough metrical gists in a notebook, and then preserve the notebook form—marginal dates, page references, colloquial

---

[2] *Histoire Générale de la Chine, ou Annales de cet Empire,* traduites du Tong-Kien-Kang-Mou, par le feu père Joseph Anne-Marie de Moyriac de Mailla, Paris, 1777-83, 12 vol. Hereafter cited as Mailla.

comments—in the text that went to the printer. Thus on page 459 of the second volume of Mailla he read this paragraph:

> Hiang-yu étoit né avec un goût décidé pour le commandement, & il ne put jamais faire le moindre progrès dans les lettres, auxquelles d'abord il avoit été destiné, & qui n'étoient utiles, disoit-il, qu'a transmettre des noms à la postérité. Il ne montra pas moins de répugnance lorsqu'on voulut lui apprendre à faire des armes, qui ne le mettoient en état que de résister à un seul homme; mais il n'en fut pas de même de l'art qui enseigne à en vaincre dix mille, dans lequel il fit les plus grands progrès. Hiang-yu avoit huit pieds de haut, & il joignoit à cette taille avantageuse une force extraordinaire de corps; mais d'ailleurs il étoit audacieux, cruel, fier, & de mauvaise foi.

After underlining "à transmettre des noms à la postérité" and making marginal pencil slashes at three other points, he sketched in a large paper-bound book labelled "Vols 1-2 Mailla"[3] this paraphrase:

>   Hiang-yu
>   with a taste
>   for commanding
>   made no progress
>   in letters
>   useful only he said
>   to transmit names to
>   posterity
>   neither wd he learn fencing—
>   but thought in terms
>   of 10 000s
>   —a giant
>   who kept no
>   faith
>   Dam'd Rhoosian
>   if you ask
>   me
>   p. 459

This is lively, like a Constable sketch. In the final text the

---

[3] I am indebted to the Princess Mary de Rachewiltz for permitting me to inspect this notebook, now at Brunnenburg.

Cover of Mrs. Pound's copy of Provença, *1910, with the poet's autograph note about the color of the cover, an undistinguished tan.*

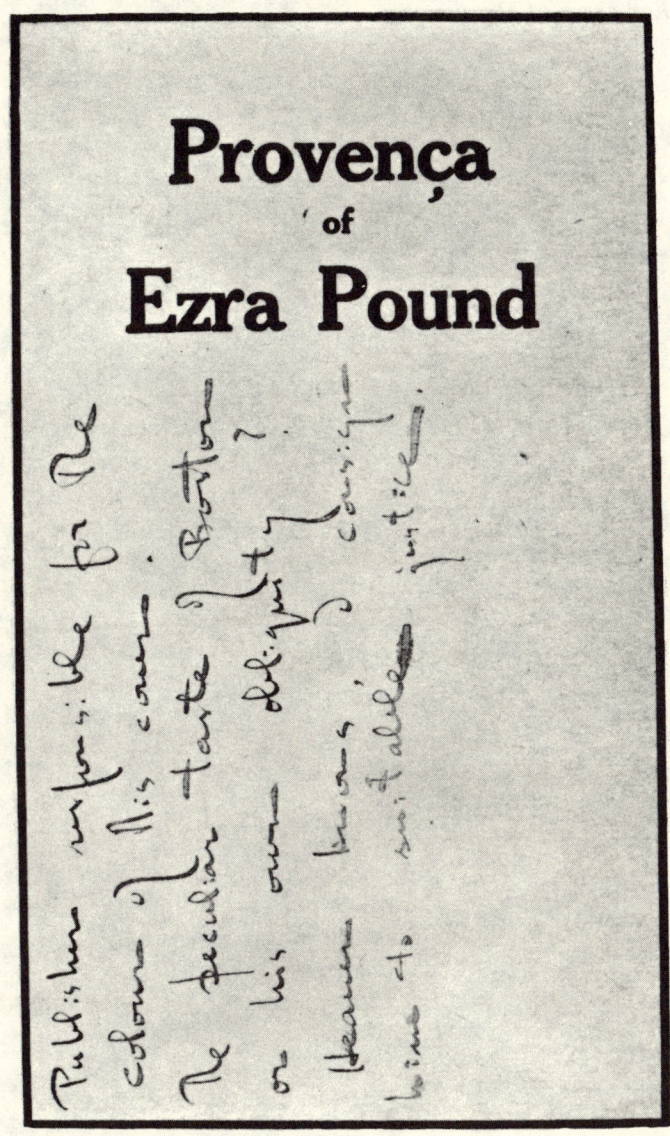

"Mistress Dorothy Shakespear": *Pound's inscription to his future wife, in her copy of* Provença.

Title page of Provença.

PROVENÇA

POEMS
SELECTED FROM PERSONAE, EXULTATIONS, AND CANZONIERE

OF

EZRA POUND

BOSTON
SMALL, MAYNARD AND COMPANY
PUBLISHERS

emphases are diminished in keeping with Hiang-yu's minor role in "Canto LIV":

> Now after the end of EULH and the death of his eunuch
> were Lieou-pang, and Hiang-yu
>   who had taste for commanding
> but made no progress in letters,
>   saying they serve only to transmit names to posterity
> and he wished to carve up the empire
>   bloody rhooshun, thought in ten thousands
> his word was worth nothing, he would not learn fencing.
>   And
>   against him....

Mailla is present in a certain decorum of phrasing and in the spelling of the proper name; as a headnote to the American printing of the sequence reminds us, "I mostly use the French form." The contemporary American asserts himself in "bloody rhooshun," the chronicle in

>   thought in ten thousands
> his word was worth nothing.

Modern Italy, except in the persistent concern with the taxonomy of strong men, is barely noticeable.

But the modern Italian setting is always present, shaping the selections and the phrases. Sometimes Pound will abandon all apparent decorum for the sake of keeping before the reader's mind the time in which this work is being done. One day in 1938 (Anno XVI) he had been condensing from Mailla the account of Han Sieun receiving the Tartar King. In "Canto LIV" this receives two-thirds of a page, concluding:

> And the next day two imperial princes went to the Prince
>   Tartar
> the Tchen-yu and brought him to the audience hall
>   where all princes sat in their orders
>   and the Tchen-yu knelt to HAN SIEUN
> and stayed three days there in festival
>   whereafter he returned to his border and province.

Having gotten that far, Pound went to the movies,[4] where a newsreel displayed certain festivals in honor of the visit to

---

[4] I owe this information to Mr. John Reid, who was in Rapallo at the time.

Italy of the modern Tartar King, Adolf Hitler. In the Bay of Naples a squadron of submarines all dived, then surfaced simultaneously. Pound's old friend Ubaldo degli Uberti, who had been a submarine commander in World War I, pronounced such a maneuver very dangerous.[5] That night Pound noted the incident opposite the Tartar King material in his Mailla notebook, with a large swastika as mnemonic of the occasion; and in the text of "Canto LIV" we read:

> (Pretty manoeuvre but the technicians
> watched with their hair standing on end
> anno sixteen, Bay of Naples)

The next item, by contrast, is dated in the margin "B.C. 49." The subject-rhyme, between Hitler's visit and the Tartar King's, has, alas, been obscured to invisibility. But "anno sixteen" retains its function; we are to recall, continually, the time when these pages were written, different from, yet in some ways possibly like, the time they were written about, and keep alert for present relevance.

We are to stay aware, in short, of a performance by a man in a particular place and time, in the presence of particular ancient models: a *mimetic homage,* shaped by person and circumstance, and not at all what is usually meant by translation or transcription. The man is what he is, or what he characterizes himself as being. The time and place guide him constantly; they are his actuality, and he is as responsible to them as to the model. The model may supply enduring ideas or enduring perception, or it may supply no more than a norm of style, as when

> Basinio left greek tags in his margin
> moulding the cadence[6]

Constantly adjusting, in his mimetic homages, the tensions of model, man and circumstance, while never allowing one of

---

[5] Information from Mrs. Dorothy Pound.

[6] "Canto CIV." Cf. *The ABC of Reading* (New York: New Directions, 1951), p. 48: "In the margins of his Latin narrative [*Issottaeus*, a poem about Sigismondo Malatesta's love for Isotta] you can still see the tags of Homer that he was using to keep his melodic sense active."

them to disappear wholly, he effects and defines the Poundian Art of Translation; for translation, once this principle is understood, becomes merely a special case of the act of writing. We can write nothing except with reference to what has been written before, if only because we cannot set down two words without stirring a whole language into life. We can write nothing except as we, whoever we may be, write it. And we cannot possibly write except here and now, and because here and now what we write seems for some reason worth the writing. Translation seems to have worried no one in the eighteenth century, when the principles of mimetic homage were still understood: a man who thought in couplets fetched from Greek what his age could use, moral exempla. It worried everyone in the nineteenth century, when, under the influence of the Holy Spirit theory, men came to hold, for the first time, that poetry at least is untranslatable; for the original poem is testimony to the moment when the Holy Spirit seized its author, an event not to be counterfeited. Having had the nerve to translate poetry in the face of this prohibition, Pound has, not unnaturally, incurred considerable abuse.

The abuse bases itself on the cult of the dictionary, an eighteenth-century invention which came to inhibit everyone by suggesting that languages were systems of equivalences. Matthew Arnold, who had the courage to examine the criteria for translating Homer in a time when such an enterprise seemed virtually impossible, was driven to posit as a norm the response of the Professor of Greek at Oxford; that translation will have succeeded, he said, which the Professor of Greek concedes has aroused in him an experience comparable to that aroused by the original. The Professor of Greek is of course a walking dictionary, his mind stuffed with Greek-English near-equivalences. Even as Arnold wrote, Liddell and Scott were cataloguing these equivalences, at Oxford, imperishably. There is really no hope of satisfying the Professor of Greek, for whom a *krēdemnon* (complete with half a column of footnotes) is something a woman of status puts on her head, *and* for whom the line

> tē de, tode krēdemnon hypo sternoio tanussai ambroton

has irreplaceable rhythmic authority, *and* for whom Odysseus and Leucothea exist at a certain inaccessible, "Hellenic," elevation. No one, except for a line or two at a time, can hope to get all those elements into English at once; and whatever element is lacking at a given instant will draw down the Professor of Greek's reproof: however pretty, not Homer.

Such difficulties are not removed, merely displaced, by the post-Arnoldian fashion of calling a poem an object, and its translation (abandoning moment-by-moment equivalence) a similar object. Each object is made of dictionary words, analyzable rhythms, identifiable systems of reference. If this fashion permits the details of each object to be referred to its own linguistic system (thus accommodating, for instance, Pound's objection that inflected and uninflected languages take different handling), it makes the question of similarity between model and translation insoluble except by way of (1) dictionary equivalences or (2) local analogies of rhetoric. What fails the former test must either be excused by the latter or dismissed as a mistake. And two elements in the three-way tension of performance are simply ignored: the person and the occasion. All attention shuttles between Original Object and Translated Object. Nobody made either object, and it was made under no circumstances in particular, but rests on our soil like a meteorite, incongruous.

Restore the person, restore the occasion, and we can talk sense. Here is the Greek, or the Latin, or the Chinese; someone like and unlike us wrote it in a time like and unlike ours. It can be read, if not by us, by someone. Here is on the other hand a somewhat similar English poem. It is the printed record of a *performance,* a mimetic homage rendered by a certain man, not concealing his traces, who in his own place and time was moved (why?) to pay in this manner his tribute to a former mastery. We are satisfied if he is true to himself and his time, and shows us that the model is one of the things that he knows, and on this occasion the preponderant thing: preponderant because relevant to what he feels and thinks here and now. He is not archaeologizing, and *bikini,* a live term in his mind now, will do for *krēdemnon.*

And translation, we have said, is a special case only. All writing rewrites what has been written, proceeds according to norms and models, chooses them, fulfills or modifies them, and does these things (if we are aware) in plain sight. Hugh Selwyn Mauberley, when he wrote his one extant poem, was sensitized to Flaubertian propaganda, half-understood. His mind, moreover, reached for analogies to the *objets d'art* among which he had spent his most alert hours; and recollecting in tranquillity the singing of Raymonde Collignon, he set down

> Luini in porcelain!

—a visual equation; and

> The sleek head emerges
> From the gold-yellow frock
> As Anadyomene in the opening
> Pages of Reinach

—another visual equation, defining not only his subject but himself and his time, his taste for art books and the British Museum Reading Room, from which his imagination is moved to bring forth its choicest treasures. His is a static homage, a *collage* of optical analogies, the rhythm tense, cluttered with hesitations, as the mind picks its careful way among scholarly exactitudes, assembling, precisely, objects into an object, grotesque (amid its pathos) as Benin statuary.

And the contrasting homage is that of "E.P.," who commences by calling it "Envoi," invoking so the presence of Chaucer and Cavalcanti, the Chaucer of the *Troilus* and the Cavalcanti of the *Ballate*. Though the poem as it rests on the page has the look of a *ballata*, and owes Cavalcanti some of its rhythmic deftness, most of the short lines turn out to be halves of iambic pentameters, the traditional English formal measure, and the opening words vary Chaucer's:

> Go, dumb-born book

Chaucer had sent forth a "litel" book, no doubt smiling as he reflected on its great length. Pound's "dumb-born" does not smile but is equally indirect. All books are dumb until a voice gives them life. This book, in fact "litel," a mere affair of twelve short poems, is as "dumb" as its contemporary subject: a new attempt, vain, people will say, "to resuscitate the dead art / Of poetry," in a time of Brennbaums, Nixons and *muflisme*.

Tell her that sang me once that song of Lawes:

The dumb thing is charged with telling; books can do that. And a new echo stirs into life:

> Go, lovely Rose,
> Tell her that wastes her time and me ...

Roses too are dumb, though lovelier than books; Waller's poem, the very song, in Lawes's setting, that Pound's lady has been singing, specifies the mimetic homage his rose is to perform: blushing, opening ("bid her come forth"), dying, in admonition to inaccessible beauty.

Waller, the rose and the lady live on in the song, reborn as often as it is sung. Pound's book offers also to build longevity for the most transient glories, those of a voice.

> Tell her that sheds
> Such treasure in the air,
> Recking naught else but that her graces give
> Life to the moment,
> I would bid them live
> As roses might, in magic amber laid,
> Red overwrought with orange and all made
> One substance and one colour
> Braving time.

In six pentameter lines printed as nine, the caesurae bringing out a precarious beauty, the great Renaissance boast, the Shakespearean boast ("braving time") is reenacted in twentieth-century London, defying earlier moods of the dumb-born book, with its "tawdry cheapness" that shall "outlast our days," and its dismissal, in Establishment accents, of attempts "to maintain 'the sublime' / in the old sense." The sublime is taking form before our ears, in a time so far declined from Waller's that the lady singing Waller's song does not know his name.

As Chaucer sent a book, and Waller a rose, so Pound once more sends a book, containing an ambered rose and terminating in a song which, one day sung, may reenact this moment for new "worshippers" as this moment reenacts so many moments gone. This art of the mimetic homage, located in time and place and stirring to new life models that will not die, is the central Poundian act. It divides itself sharply from Mauberley's "Medallion," the small carved thing exquisite but voiceless, exposed to vicissitudes of taste and cut off from the reality it would celebrate by insisting on visual analogies in the presence of auditory fact. The poesis of objects strikes out after a specious immortality, like Ignez de Castro's,

>   Seated there,
>   dead eyes,
>   Dead hair under the crown.

Homage by mimesis, the act of a living man, as often as it is repeated, can bring life.

CRAFT AND MORALS

by A. Alvarez

This essay was written ten years ago, when I was fresh from university and Pound was still held in St. Elizabeth's Hospital. I visited him there twice and saw him in both his personae.

The first time we met alone and talked about literature. He was witty, courteous, lucid, passionately interesting and interested, a devoted master of poetry who, in the locked, evil-smelling ward of a mental hospital, looked perilously like becoming a latter-day martyr to the subject.

When I went back a couple of days later, he was surrounded by disciples and was talking politics. They were pumping him on currency reform, "Commie plots" and the use of drugs for political ends. His talk was rhetorical, disorganized and full of improbable theories. At moments he gave the impression of being faintly embarrassed by his followers' zeal. Otherwise there seemed little connection between this tired man droning on about usury and the dedicated, vigorous, eminently intelligent man of letters I'd seen a couple of days before.

If the second visit was, in comparison, unpleasant and depressing, it was also sad. No doubt Pound had, to some extent, wished those young political hoods on himself. Yet the fact is that, apart from the usual bevy of scholars, they were the only ones who were willing to put themselves out to visit him regularly. He gave off a sense of terrible loneliness, and also of great courage and resilience. Although I felt uneasily that he would probably not have seen me at the time had he known I was a Jew, he seemed equally to deserve some kind of tribute for the horrors he was being made to put up with.

The poetry that came out of this bad time—the Pisan Cantos *and* Rock-Drill—*was often as fine as anything he'd done since the opening of the* Cantos. *It was as though his verse were rising to the crisis of his despair. Now his imprisonment in the mental hospital has become merely part of his long, eighty-year history; the poetry has correspondingly become less interesting, less urgent. Thrones was disappointing: programmatic, hectoring, scrappy. Instead of pulling the* Cantos *together and concentrating his art for a great final poetic synthesis, he seems to be letting them run out into a shallow delta of cross-references and Pound scholarship. By coming through that long nightmare in Washington more or less intact he scored a great personal triumph. But the chances, I think, of the* Cantos *being an equal poetic triumph have become more and more remote. They remain an ambiguous monument to a highly ambiguous figure. I still stand by my original essay.*

1965

POUND, more than Whitman, Emily Dickinson or even Eliot, is the first really American poet; the first, that is, who, despite all the literary machinery of his verse, has nothing to do with the tradition of English poetry. His Americanism, of course, involves much that is beyond the scope of this essay. In recent years he has, for instance, become its victim: his obstinate insistence that he is free to hold whatever political opinions he pleases has led to his ten-year confinement in a mental hospital. And Pound's importance as a figure on the American scene does owe something to the fact that he is, so far as I know, the first major artist to be held as a political prisoner since the Nazis took Alban Berg. I will have nothing to say here of Pound as a person. This essay was drafted before I met him; although I have altered a number of details since then, the critical judgments on which it is based remain unchanged.

American scholars are much given to tinkering with Pound's machinery. The English Institute, for example, met in 1953 to discuss him in great seriousness and detail; he is the sole subject of a solemn periodical, the *Pound Newsletter;* and Mr. John J. Espey has recently come forward with a long investigation of *Mauberley,* done in the manner and with much of the thoroughness of Lowes's *The Road to Xanadu*. Although much of the work is admirable and, in Mr. Espey's book, illuminating, although some of it is even necessary, Pound is in danger of being swallowed up by his researchers. Under it all the original poetic voice is easily lost.

In England, on the other hand, it has hardly been heard. Pound is accorded the weary applause due to a man who, whatever else he achieves, is important in literary history: he gave Eliot his start, and Joyce, and Wyndham Lewis; he helped Yeats find his colloquial strength; he is, as Mr. Eliot has remarked, "the inventor of Chinese poetry for our time," and also that of Provence; his critical tips are still current; finally, by tightening up the language and making sensitive the rhythms of verse, Pound is literally the inventor of the accepted medium of modern poetry. Despite all this, he is very little read. Of the thousand-odd pages of his poetry, only *Mauberly, Propertius* and "The Seafarer" are common property; add a few lyrics and epigrams and some fragments of the Cantos, the rest goes virtually unopened. Perhaps this is inevitable in a poet of Pound's output: the sheer bulk of its tells against him; the reader can only select. But I think with Pound the selection has been done by a very few enthusiasts; the readers rarely hunt for themselves. In England the Cantos are probably as little read and even less theorized on than *Finnegan's Wake*. It is not merely the bulk of the writing that is forbidding, it is the unwieldy masses of oddly assorted learning with which Pound has stuffed it, and his cheery assurance that his readers will, with the least formality, get acquainted with the intimate details of his reading and associations. There is something of a Daisy Miller in the poet of parts of the Cantos.

There is too a kind of irritating awkwardness with the tradition, even when his writing and his influence bring him closest to it. Set against his immediate predecessors and against most of their Victorian forebears, Pound is artistically puritanical yet colloquial, serious, original, vigorous, straight. Those qualities in him and in Eliot have made the present poetic continuum wider and deeper than it was. It has made us aware of something which is, in fact, very different: the independence, naturalness and intimate offhand intelligence of the seventeenth-century poets. But Pound seems to have come at those qualities indirectly and, to judge from his earliest volumes, almost despite himself. His pronouncements on English poetry are uncertain, sporadic and biased. He has come forward with some extraordinary statements in his time. For instance, in 1927 he wrote of four classes of poets; the lowest was:

> The men who do more or less good work in the more or less good style of a period. Of these the delightful anthologies, the song books, and choice among them is a matter of taste, for you prefer Wyatt to Donne, Donne to Herrick, Drummond of Hawthornden to Browne, in response to some purely personal sympathy, these people add but some slight personal flavour, some minor variant of a mode, without affecting the main course of the story.
> ("How to Read")

My instincts tell me he doesn't know what he is talking about. Then I remember that this was published ten years after *Propertius,* seven after *Mauberley;* they are both testament enough that he knew very well. Putting aside trivial reasons for this aberration (at forty-one he would hardly have felt the need to shock; but he *may* only have read these authors as they appear in the songbooks), it seems that Pound, when he wants to, is capable of an extraordinary singlemindedness in his reading. He has a wonderful ear for verse and a firm conviction that the true art of singing had been lost in English poetry in effect since Chaucer ("Shakespeare as supreme lyric technician is indebted to the Italian song-books, but they are already EXOTIC," *The ABC of Reading*). And so he set himself to revive our sensitivity to the music of words: his first translation of *Donna Mi Prega* has a *"Dedicace*—To Thomas Campion his ghost, and to the ghost of Henry Lawes, as prayer for the revival of music." He seems to have devoted himself so wholly to his task that he could read with all his critical attention not exactly on the sound of the thing but on something that needed more brain work, the technique of the sound.

Caring so much for this, he seems hardly to have bothered with the tones of meaning, or, as in his sideswipe at Donne, with originality which enlarged the whole range of experience possible in verse.

And yet he produced *Mauberley*, which, Dr. Leavis said, has "a subtlety of tone, a complexity of attitude, such as we associate with seventeenth-century wit." Although he did so without, as it appears, any clear idea of the native English tradition, or of seventeenth-century poetry, he did not come to it unprepared. His real flair and insight was for the poetry of other languages. The sophisticated intelligence of *Mauberley*, its ironical use of learning and the deflating cliché, the apparent colloquialisms where every word is, in fact, scrupulously weighed, derive not from, say, Marvell, but from Laforgue and Corbière. What Pound found in them, Eliot praised in the Metaphysicals. They went at it from different ends—one admiring the skill, the other the wholeness and honesty of the response—but they finished with the same standards of accomplishment. Mr. Espey's book shows how much *Mauberley* derives from Gautier in its ideal of the chasteness of language, in its references and images. I feel he underestimates the pervading influence of Laforgue on the tone. But it hardly matters. The important point remains: Pound wrote one of his few major works that has been generally acclaimed, in which he comes closest to a vital and difficult English tradition, at the moment when he was modeling himself most closely on French poetry.

This, I think, is a general rule for Pound's work, not an exception: he is at his best when most actively putting the strengths of another language into English—which is something quite different from the moments when he tries to write English and fails. As an example, I would like to set an early translation of *Propertius* against a section from the *Homage* (Mr. Kenner has used these two poems, but to make different points):

Here let thy clemency, Persephone, hold firm,
Do thou, Pluto, bring here no greater harshness.

So many thousand beauties are gone down to Avernus.
Ye might let one remain above with us.

With you is Iope, with you the white-gleaming Tyro,
With you is Europa and the shameless Pasiphae,
And all the fair from Troy and all the Achaia,
From the sundered realms, of Thebes and of aged Priamus;
And all the maidens of Rome, as many as they were,
They died and the greed of your flame consumes them.
(Personae, 1908, '09, '10)

Persephone and Dis, Dis, have mercy upon her,
There are quite enough women in hell,
          quite enough beautiful women,
Iope, and Tyro, and Pasiphae, and the formal girls of
  Achaia,
And out of Troad, and from the Campania,
Death has his tooth in the lot,
          Avernus lusts for the lot of them,
Beauty is not eternal, no man has perennial fortune,
Slow foot, or swift foot, death delays but for a season.
(Homage to Sextus Propertius, 1917)

In the early version Pound is out to translate the words, no matter what; even at the expense of the English itself. Archaisms jostle with coy periphrases ("Ye might let one remain above with us"); lines are padded with expressions that do not exist outside translators' dialect ("as many as they were"); there are awkward inversions. The later poem is not so much a translation as variations on a theme by Propertius. Pound does in English what the Latin poet had done in his own language: he uses the resources of the language to its full, creating new, individual rhythms which are not those of Propertius, yet give a taste to the verse which is not quite English. They are the outcome of his critical reading of Propertius. By that I don't merely mean that Pound discovered the irony in Propertius and created from him yet another *persona*. It is something in a way more thoroughgoing. He is literally writing Latin verse in English, using the same quality of language as we find in Propertius—colloquial, resonant or ironic—and using it in what is basically a Latin meter:

> There are quite enough women in hell,
> 		quite enough beautiful women . . .
> Death has his tooth in the lot,
> 		Avernus lusts for the lot of them . . .

These are both more or less regular elegiac pentameters—less regular only because they have been accommodated to the cadence of the English idiom. So much has Pound made the Latin verse his own that the foreign quantitative meter emphasizes the native speaking emphasis; for example, in the first line the caesura is used to administer the ironic shock of the unexpected word "hell." Certainly, *Propertius*, like *Mauberley*, is also an ironic survey of Pound's own time and place; in it the Roman becomes curiously modern:

> Annalists will continue to record Roman reputations,
> Celebrities from the Trans-Caucasus will belaud Roman
> 	celebrities
> And expound the distentions of Empire,
> But for something to read in normal circumstances?
> For a few pages brought down from the forked hills
> 	unsullied?
> I ask a wreath that will not crush my head.
> 		And there is no hurry about it;
> I shall have, doubtless, a boom after my funeral,
> Seeing that long standing increases all things
> 			regardless of quality.

It is this that gives him that resilience and intelligent sense of proportion which reminded Dr. Leavis of the seventeenth-century poets; they too were soaked in classical literature. The difference is that Pound does not, as most modern poets might, get at the Latin through the seventeenth century. He seems to work directly through the foreign language. And this is the essence of his best writing. It owes its freshness and economy to this power of using words as if he had just coined them. His language has no literary incrustations. He is the only poet in the last three hundred years to write English as though he had never read Shakespeare. For with Shakespeare the English language crystallized out. The imaginative fullness, the power and flexibility of Shakespeare's verse have been the abiding fact for every subsequent major poet. His originality and strength are what is left to him after he has fought it out with Shakespeare. But Pound has had no part in that fight. When I suggested this to him, he replied that his literary ancestor was Dante. He has, in fact, struggled with translation and with the business of writing verse to foreign plans. Yet it has left him a language that is curiously his own, curiously undisturbed by the English tradition that preceded it. It is for this that I have called him the first really American poet.

His achievement depends directly on his ability as a translator, or, more accurately, on his growing intimacy with the poetry of other languages and the skill with which he adapted their techniques to English. Pound has two poems in *The Oxford Book of Victorian Verse,* and they sit there not at all uncomfortably. In the very beginning he, like Yeats, was not set apart from the members of the Rhymers' Club by any startling originality of mind or truth to feeling. But he was energetic and devoted; he was willing to give himself wholly to the sheer hard grind of discovering, reviving and putting into practice the art of using language to its fullest. What there was to hand at the turn of the century was useless; the language had grown loose and nerveless, since it was never called on to perform more than the dullest and most habitual tasks. So again and again Pound went to other literatures. His gradual advance from the Browning-and-haze of *Personae,* 1908, '09, '10, to *Ripostes,* 1912; *Lustra,* 1915, and finally *Mauberley* in 1920 is the outcome of the continual effort and discipline of translation. His *Cavalcanti* appeared in 1912; so did "The Seafarer"; *Cathay,* the paraphrases of Fenollosa's notes, came out in 1915; the *Noh* plays in 1916; *Homage to Sextus Propertius* in 1917; and the *Arnaut Daniel Poems,* which in the accompanying technical essay he said he had been at work on for ten years, were printed in 1920. The translations, in fact, were the "ground bass" of his most productive period, which culminated in *Propertius, Mauberley* and the earliest Cantos.

The difference between the early and the later volumes

is more than skill—although now the epigrams are interesting chiefly for what they led to; it took practice in

> Her two cats
> Go before her into Avernus;
> A sort of chloroformed suttee. . . .
> ("The Social Order, II," *Lustra*)

to achieve the speed and polish of *Mauberley's* "Dowson found harlots cheaper than hotels." Often the early poems seem skillfully enough done, but the skill seems to dissipate itself into the air; he has so little to say. Translation presented more than the technical problem of finding the exact words; it provided Pound with ready-made occasions for writing, upon which his very real feeling for literature could come into play. At his best, other literature is always an *occasion* for Pound. Instead of translating word for word, he seems to get on the inside of a work and re-create it outward. His translations seem to me more original and more personal than those poems in which he has only himself to rely on. In *Ripostes,* for example, is a piece which Mr. Eliot has praised in his Introduction to the *Selected Poems*. It is of arguable but rather typical merit:

> "A Girl"
> The tree has entered my hands,
> The sap has ascended my arms,
> The tree has grown in my breasts—
> Downward,
> The branches grow out of me, like arms.
>
> Tree you are,
> Moss you are,
> You are violets with wind above them.
> A child—*so* high—you are,
> And all this is folly to the world.

"There, you see," says Mr. Eliot, "the 'feeling" is original in the best sense, but the phrasing is not quite "completed"; for the last line is one which I or half a dozen other men might have written. Yet it is not 'wrong,' and I certainly could not improve upon it." I feel Mr. Eliot is too modest and rather too involved in his inverted commas. I am not at all sure how original the "feeling" is. The young girl as a tree, the stripling, is after all something of a cliché. What originality there is lies in the way Pound has elaborated it into a sort of late-Victorian conceit. But whether the impulse is a flickering mood or whether it is ingenuity, he seems not to know what to do with it. Far from "completed," the last stanza has been faked: Wordsworth's "violet by a mossy stone" is half-hidden in it. It is literary, in the bad, the tricksy-tricksy, sense.

The same image and something of the same intention recur in *Mauberley*, but this time in the form of a quotation:

> "Daphne with her thighs in bark
> Stretches toward me her leafy hands,"—
> Subjectively. In the stuffed-satin drawing-room
> I await The Lady Valentine's commands,
>
> Knowing my coat has never been
> Of precisely the fashion
> To stimulate, in her,
> A durable passion;

Mr. Espey has pointed out that these first two lines are from Gautier's "Le Château du Souvenir":

> Daphné, les hanches dans l'écorce,
> Etend toujours ses doigts touffus;
> Mais aux bras du dieu qui la force
> Elle s'eteint, spectre confus.

The "feeling" for the Lady Valentine may perhaps be less "original" than in "A Girl"; it is certainly sharper and more alive. The attraction, the mood, is seen in the round: real but one-sided ("Subjectively") and a little grotesque (the shabby poet is a long way from "le dieu qui la force"). Yet at the same time the Lady in her "stuffed-satin drawing-room" falls far short of his ideal of pagan sensual grace. They are all judged, the poet and his mood, Lady Valentine and her circumstances, through the quotation. It voices the poet's feelings at the same time as it allows him to step outside and examine them in perspective. In *Mauberley* there is the mood and the play of mind upon it, where in the first poem there was only a play of words.

Pound on his own, in fact, is not particularly full. Pound working through other literature is. He needs the framework of translation. It keeps his intellect and imagination at full stretch by providing for all the technical business while he sustains his understanding of the poem and the poet. Within those limits he recreates the feeling for himself. As a poet he moves, thinks and feels with the greatest ease and strength in other men's clothes.

TWO

Pound's superb craftsman's intelligence seems then not quite geared to what he feels outside literature; as though his response to experience as he lived it were not inadequate, but of a different order to the technical subtlety at his command. For me, one of the main troubles with the Cantos[1] is not their obscurity but their remoteness. They refuse to fix themselves with any sort of inevitability. Again and again there are passages of great beauty, but they are remote, done for their own sakes; the poet himself seems hardly to exist. Even the finest Cantos have this evasive, centerless quality. A number of moments from literature, each recreated in its own terms, are held together by a loose flow of association and a tenuous theme which the reader himself must supply. "Canto II," for example, culminates in a long translation-paraphrase of the third book of Ovid's *Metamorphoses:*

> And where was gunwale, there now was vine-trunk,
>   and tenthril where cordage had been,
>   grape-leaves on the rowlocks
> Heavy vine on the oarshafts,
> And, out of nothing, a breathing,
>   hot breath on my ankles,
> Beasts like shadows in glass,
>   a furred tail upon nothingness.

[1] That is, Cantos I-LXXIII. I discuss the *Pisan Cantos* in the final section of this essay.

> Lynx-purr, and heathery smell of beasts,
>   where tar smell had been,
> Sniff and pad-foot of beasts,
>   eye-glitter out of black air.
> The sky overshot, dry, with no tempest....

The whole passage—there are three pages of it—is an extraordinary *tour de force;* the choice of clear, strange details coupled with the chanting rhythm, again based on the Latin meter, sets the scene in a hard, dry, powerful light. Yet it remains, most persuasively, an artistic performance. The language is so impeccable that it will not stretch itself to do a jot more than its immediate job. When language is, to use Pound's definition of great literature, "charged with meaning to the utmost possible degree," it radiates out from its situation, forcing the reader back into his own experience, not to complete the verse, but to add to it, as a boulder gathers mass with momentum. Pound's language stays on the page; its accuracy and economy guard the reader against going any further than the single poetic moment. Each passage seems isolated, self-contained, almost ornamental.

Yet they are strangely moving. For all their remoteness they have a powerful existence of their own, though it almost never touches earth. It is partly a matter of the clarity of the writing and the extraordinary accuracy of the detail. And partly the care that these entail; it seems to come from something deeper than the apparent disconnectedness suggests. Behind it is a sort of awe of the past and of its literature, a belief that these things have, in Pound's contemporary cultural wasteland, an inherent value of their own. It is this passionate antiquarianism which invests the remote with a queer, moving force, and yet, with an equal passion, preserves its remoteness. For all their scope, the Cantos are very specialized poetry.

Pound has always technique at his command, even when he is using it to be aggressively unpoetic, busily transcribing historical documents or even, at moments, pastiching Ring Lardner. His style is as adequate to his whim as to his sober purposes. This is why the Cantos are never really difficult: he says what he wants very skillfully, and he never has anything very difficult to say. "Ash Wednesday" is obscure because it demands so much of the reader; preconceptions and obfuscations have to be stripped away in order to follow the delicate unfeigned shifts of feeling and argument. In the Cantos I find myself often at a loss for the reference; I want to know who the characters are, what books he is referring to, quoting from, paraphrasing. Their obscurity, in fact, is largely in the keeping of a competent editor.

But not quite. The other difficulty is more insoluble: weighing against his artistic concentration is Pound's inveterate garrulousness. The Cantos have too much in them. Keeping his own purposes so much in the background and excited by the past and the remote, it is enough that one thing should lead to another. "The secret of his form is this:" said Allen Tate, "conversation. *The Cantos* are talk, talk, talk. . . .The length of breath, the span of conversational energy, is the length of a Canto. The conversationalist pauses; there is just enough unfinished business left hanging in the air to give him a new start; so that the transitions between the Cantos are natural and easy." The transitions within the Cantos, however, are far from easy. They seem to depend on nothing more than what Pound happens to think of next. So, for all the impersonality, the poet demands of the reader a considerable trust, as he leads him blindfold through his complicated maze of literary facts and figures.

Commentators on the Cantos warn continually against reading for the plot. They substitute a host of technical theories; they quote Pound's hint to Yeats on the permutation of themes and figures. But Yeats was notoriously gullible; he seems to have been overcome by the grandness of the gesture, "scribbled on the back of an envelope," for it is meagerly justified in the Cantos as they stand. The general theme of the work is clear enough: the quest for civilization and the descent into corruption of a number of societies and times, classical, Renaissance, Chinese, American, contemporary. But that is so large that it brings the reader no nearer than to be told that in *Finnegan's Wake* a man is born, lives, copulates, dies. Both works, by their careful surface detail, seem to offer something more complicated and exact.

We are told to read not for the plot but between the lines—Hugh Kenner, in *The Poetry of Ezra Pound*, has suggested that Pound has erected the scaffolding with great care and deliberately left out the bricks. Pound himself says that the Cantos are built up like a fugue: themes and phrases recur; nearly all the women, for example, turn out in time to be Circe. By attending patiently to the details the drift of the thing will eventually appear. But theories, technical details, even artistic accomplishment run into the ground too soon in a long poem. The singleness of Pound's devotion to the craft of poetry and his ideal of the impersonality of art seem, when extended over six hundred-odd pages, to dissipate interest instead of focusing it. The work has the hustle of artistic life, but not its inevitability. It is full of names, figures and actions; but the abiding central life of the artist judging and ordering the details, creating them in his own coherence, is not there. For all their energy and invention, their vividness and detail, despite even the devotion with which each is rendered, the Cantos suffer from their size and inclusiveness. It is hard to see how they "contain in themselves the reason why they are so and not otherwise." The final impression is less of artistic impersonality than of considerable casualness.

There is, in fact, a split between what is said and how it is said, between a Flaubertian preoccupation with style and a randomness in marshalling the materials of the poem which reminds me of no method so much as the late Senator McCarthy's. For example, even in the famous Canto against usury, XLV, the feeling and the words are not quite one:

WITH USURA
wool comes not to market
sheep bringeth no gain with usura
Usura is a murrain, usura
blunteth the needle in the maid's hand

and stoppeth the spinner's cunning. Pietro Lombardo
came not by usura
Duccio came not by usura
nor Pier della Francesca; Zuan Bellin' not by usura
nor was "La Calunnia" painted.
Came not by usura Angelico; came not Ambrogio Praedis,
Came no church of cut stone signed: *Adamo me fecit.*
Not by usura St Trophime
Not by usura Saint Hilaire,
Usura rusteth the chisel
It rusteth the craft and the craftsman
It gnaweth the thread in the loom
None learneth to weave gold in her pattern;
Azure hath a canker by usura; cramoisi is unbroidered
Emerald findeth no Memling
Usura slayeth the child in the womb
It stayeth the young man's courting
It hath brought palsey to bed, lyeth
Between the young bride and her bridegroom
                    CONTRA NATURA
They have brought whores for Eleusis
Corpses are set to banquet
at behest of usura.

It is powerful writing, but its success relies on the flow of biblical denunciation, not on the logic of the examples. The Canto has its sanction from Dante, for whom usury was also a sin against Nature and Art:

> Da queste due, se tu ti rechi a mente
>   lo Genesi dal principio, conviene
>   prender sua vita ed avanzar la gente.
> E perchè l'usuriere altra via tiene,
>   per sè natura, e per la sua seguace
>   dispregia, poichè in altro pon la spene.
>   *(Inferno,* XI, 106-11)

Compared with Pound's these lines are flat; but they are reasoned, they follow out the idea. Pound ornaments it. His thought and feeling are static and separate. On one side is the rage against usury, *contra naturam;* on the other are examples of fruitfulness and culture. He writes as though there were a causal connection between the two, but in fact it exists only in his beliefs. And these remain simple; they are neither modified nor developed in the verse. The common ground between the belief and the examples is their appropriateness to the biblical style. The detail of the verse is elaborate and carefully wrought; the feeling is very simple.

It is this unquestioning, static quality in his beliefs that allows Pound to be satisfied at times with a surprising emotional rough-and-readiness. His inferno, for example, Cantos XIV and XV, hardly moves beyond darkness, defecation and anger. Although Dame Edith Sitwell has announced that "such lines as

> Flies carrying news, harpies dripping shit through the air

are great poetry, and a living evocation of the modern hell," I cannot see this as a Vision of Evil. It seems to me much nearer Naughtiness. It is shocking, but it is not tragic, not moral; it is nothing that involves Pound himself whether he likes it or not; it is as Henry James described Hawthorne's sense of sin: "He was not discomposed, disturbed, haunted by it in the manner of its usual and regular victims, who had not the little postern door of fancy to slip through, to the other side of the wall." For long stretches of the Cantos Pound holds his beliefs almost in the teeth of his poetry. He strikes a number of compromising and aggressive postures in some of the most highly disciplined and elaborate poetry of our time. It is a combination so odd that it makes the poem doubly difficult to interpret. Pound uses the ideogram: he presents isolated images, facts and anecdotes, and allows them to speak for themselves. It is left to the reader to fill in the empty spaces between them. The poet roughly insists on one interpretation; the sophisticated performance hints at another.

Hence the uneasiness of Pound's critics; it has forced them to defend the Cantos by slipping into explication and commentary, by pointing to the good bits and lamenting that every long poem has dull moments, or by pretending, as Mr. Eliot has done, that it does not matter what Pound says; what counts is the way he says it. It seems to me that it matters very much, for it is precisely this split between belief and performance that has caused the critical shiftiness in the writing on Pound. There are two accepted masterpieces, *Mauberley* and *Propertius;* there are, I think, the equally acceptable first seven Cantos; and then disagreement. I cannot believe that there was any drastic change in Pound's sensibility in the early 'twenties. What happened was more consistent: he has ridden two high horses during his career, one of them popular, the other not; one had to do with cultural and poetic standards, the other was economic. I said his beliefs are simply, unquestionably held; which is to say that he has always been a writer with a cause, up to 1920 no less than after. His first cause was poetic. When he arrived in England the language and rhythms of verse were so dulled and worn they were unusable. He set about to reform them by bringing back the old standards of "Mediterranean civilization" (his phrase); these were calm, objective, rounded off and stringent. By them he could counteract both the Rhymers' self-indulgence and the utter indifference of his own "half-savage country." And in these standards he had the same absolute trust as he later put in his social remedies; even in *Mauberley* he contrasts modern Fleet Street with Dr. Johnson's in a way which the author of *The Vanity of Human Wishes* would have been hard put to understand. Though the deepened, subtle tone of *Mauberley* and *Propertius* comes from the clash between belief and disenchantment, belief, in the end, won. What is so moving in the opening Cantos is the sense of reverence for the cultures they evoke. Pound's energy and enthusiasm brought about his reform; he made modern poetry possible.

So he turned his attention elsewhere; economic passion replaced the cultural. When he campaigned for poetic standards he did so most effectively by writing well. When he turned to social abuses he used his verse as a vehicle for propaganda. The performance was no longer so inherently important. He developed a slangy, irreverent style to force over the facts. Hence the long, dull sections on Chinese and American history, Cantos LIII-LXXI, which read as though he had gone through his sources marking the bits that mattered, had gathered his findings together, but never subsequently digested them into poetry. Yet it is done with the same unwavering belief in the value of his cause. It is a belief shared by few. So the reader is constantly uneasy about what Pound will come out with next, as his sense of literature is overwhelmed by the mass of facts and theories. For his gifts are not economic; they are literary and intuitive. His most expressive form is the short poem. Both *Mauberley* and *Propertius* are a series of these; the finest parts of the Cantos have the same singleness and concentration. His social reforming zeal lacks the inwardness and sense of purpose that give inevitability to a long work. In fact, the Cantos fail precisely when they come nearest to being a traditional long poem, when they are didactic. For the dogma he preaches and the suggestiveness of the ideogrammic method strain impossibly against each other. It is like playing a hymn-tune on a clavichord.

THREE

The *Pisan Cantos* are unlike Pound's other work because they were written not without a cause but from the failure of all his causes. Where in *Mauberley* and *Propertius* belief clashes with disenchantment, in the *Pisan Cantos* it disintegrates in despair. They were written when Pound was brought from his life of secluded dedication in Rapallo and put into the condemned cages at Pisa, where neither style nor theories would protect him. The result is the most extended personal verse Pound has ever written. It is personal in two ways: it is about his experiences and memories; it is also, in places, not wholly a public poem. These two elements have a great deal to do with each other. The middle sections of the Cantos read like a scrapbook in which much poetic material has been pasted, some with great care, some with abandon. The *Pisan Cantos* are a sort of poetic journal. The hard surface of art and fact is broken down from ideogram into tiny shards of verse in which the perennial themes of the poem jostle with memories, with details of his life in the cages and with bleak level judgments on himself:

> J'ai eu pitié des autres
> probablement pas assez, and at moments that suited my own convenience
> Le paradis n'est pas artificiel,
> l'enfer non plus.
> Came Eurus as comforter
> and at sunset la pastorella dei suini
> driving the pigs home, benecomata dea.
> (LXXXVI)

The *Pisan Cantos* are a remarkable achievement. In them Pound has moments of real impersonality: he writes of his own personal tragedy with an utter lack of self-pity. But, though it may seem a grudging verdict, they are a limited achievement; they are essentially not understandable as a whole. Their general order is that of Pound's day-to-day life, but their logic is the drift of his most intimate associations; it is fully available only to Pound himself. Even the ideogram breaks down, for the facts do not speak for themselves. The *Pisan Cantos,* for example, abound with names:

> and Demattia is checking out.
>   White, Fazzio, Bedell, *benedicti*
> Sarnone, two Washingtons (dark) J and M
>   Bassier, Starcher, H. Crowder and
> no soldier he although his name is Slaughter
> this day October the whateverth   Mr. Coxie
> aged 91 has mentioned bonds and their
>   interest
>   apparently as a basis of issue. . .
> (LXXXIV)

None of these people are made up; Pound has repeatedly stated that he is not writing fiction in the Cantos. So the reader is supposed not merely to recognize them—the first lot are presumably soldiers at the camp—but to reckon up their significance. Yet Pound makes no attempt to give them any imaginative reality through action and detail. They never disengage themselves from his memories and step into the public creative world. I feel that when he abandoned *personae* and formalism he still did not achieve artistic nakedness. There is instead a despairing fragmentariness to these Cantos. It is as though the artistic habit were so engrafted onto him that he could avoid it only by a kind of disintegration. In the *Pisan Cantos* there is no longer any question of the life and the love being only in the learning; his effort is to make past and present, memory, experience and learning, into a living whole which will sum up the whole work. But it is the bewildering effort that comes through clearest. He succeeds in writing personally only by doing violence to the technicalities which had previously sustained him. Yet the success in certain passages is of an order he has not attained since 1920:

> The ant's a centaur in his dragon world.
> Pull down thy vanity, it is not man
> Made courage, or made order, or made grace,
>   Pull down thy vanity, I say pull down.
> Learn of the green world what can be thy place
> In scaled invention or true artistry,
> Pull down thy vanity,
>   Paquin pull down!
> The green casque has outdone your elegance.
>
> "Master thyself, then others shall thee beare"
>   Pull down thy vanity
> Thou art a beaten dog beneath the hail,
> A swollen magpie in a fitful sun,
> Half black half white
> Nor knowst'ou wing from tail
> Pull down thy vanity
>   How mean thy hates
> Fostered in falsity,
>   Pull down thy vanity,
> Rathe to destroy, niggard in charity,
> Pull down thy vanity,
>   I say pull down.
>   (LXXXI)

The whole conclusion of the Canto—I have quoted only a

fragment—is some of the finest sustained personal verse that Pound has ever done. It is written too with the same air of discovery he had in his earlier verse. The thought again is quite simple, but it has dignity and power. It is as though in the *Pisan Cantos* Pound were breaking through the restrictions of craft to a personal morality for which his earlier preoccupation with causes had never left time. And it makes those causes seem very thin diet. The triumph of his sense of literature has been that here, in *Mauberley* and in *Propertius,* Pound's own finest achievements have been to write the epitaphs on his own poetic genre.

EZRA POUND AND CATULLUS

by Peter Whigham

> *I would much rather lie on what is left of Catullus' parlour floor and speculate the azure beneath it and the hills off to Salò and Riva with their forgotten gods moving unhindered amongst them than discuss any processes and theories of art whatsoever.*
>
> *A Retrospect (1918)*
>
> *One might do worse than open a pub on Lake Garda . . . .*
> *"Canto LXXVIII"*

WHEN SANTAYANA emerged from his wartime isolation with a short autobiographical piece published in Cyril Connolly's *Horizon,* he found occasion to quote the well-known line *glubit magnanimi Remi nepotes,* from poem 58 of Catullus' *Carmina.* It would appear that in the disorder and degradation of military occupation he had witnessed—presumably beyond the confines of San Stefano—scenes similar to that described by Catullus. I cannot remember whether or not Ezra Pound had already made use of the same line in "Canto LXXIV." Even if he had, it would not have been the reason for my writing to him. I had recently translated poem 58 (my work on the *Carmina* dates back as far as that), and while the actual meaning of the line in question was perfectly plain, there were doubts about the traditional interpretation which I had chosen to give it. Peter Russell, who was then running his successful magazine, *Nine*, was unsure whether this interpretation was justified. He urged me to write to Ezra Pound. "He'll be sure to have something to say," Russell told me. "And whatever it is it's bound to be interesting, and will probably be very funny." It was. Having first confirmed the justness of Santayana's quotation and my reading, he went on to give—as he has never been able to refrain from giving—more than was asked of him. He was unable, he wrote, to recall the vicinage at San Stefano whence he (Santayana) could have observed very exactly, but reckoned that "old Jarge must have been leanin' over the fence an' usin' a pair of opry glarses." As so often, the unlooked-for comment proved an inimitable enrichment. I am now totally incapable of reading poem 58 without at the same time picturing the Olympian, if slightly prim, Santayana thus incongruously engaged. It was not until many years later that I learned that Santayana's sense of humor was far more lively about such matters than those who did not know him very well would ever have suspected—that he was not, in fact, half as prim as he let on. Pound's fantasy had point.

There is a mystique about Catullus that there is not about any other of the great Roman poets. The elements are comparatively easy to single out, but the special nature of the mystique is something more than their sum. There is Sappho and Greek poetry in Roman dress; Lesbia, and the ability to make exquisitely turned *nugae* out of the furniture of everyday life; there is the dislike of important official people like Julius Caesar; there is Lake Garda, Sirmio, the yacht drawn up under the terrace; there are vitriolic fantasies, and there is tenderness and the personal note in poetry which is still (except for two or three poems) saved from the confessional.

Nearly all these elements appear in various forms in the middle section of Pound's *Personae* (1926), while the mystique, as an atmosphere, is present throughout. When Pound speaks of a work of art creating its own ambience, he naturally intends the statement to be taken aesthetically.

But an artist will in some sense shed his influence over his material surroundings also. A poem or a picture, not unlike the somewhat grisly relics of which we read in pious books, is capable of imparting something of its aura to whomever or whatever it has been associated with. And no one is more sensitive to the effect of this association than Ezra Pound. People have been too ready to take the appearance of austere iconoclasm at more than face value. For the most part, it has been little more than a way of getting a certain point across. To those who are willing to read between the lines, or who know him, his tastes are catholic and not particularly austere. His piety toward anything associated with what he considers a noble human achievement is active and personal. The associative links in the Cantos are evidence of this. But they are not more so than the nature of the Catullan references in the early poems.

While this is a tribute to Pound's sense of poetic *pietas,* and explains why, over the question of the *tradition* of a line of poetry, I should so naturally have turned to him, it is not without irony; for the discernible influence that Catullus had on his early poetry was probably not what Pound himself either anticipated or sought. But then he would have been something more than human if this had not been so.

It is well known that round about 1914-16 Pound, Hulme, Ford and others were of the opinion that English verse was in need of certain qualities, such as hardness, clarity and directness, which are usually associated with epigrammatic technique. Some poets, such as H. D., turned to Greek models. Pound himself did so in some of his loveliest pieces. But he suspected that something sparser than even what the Greeks had to offer, a sparseness without necessarily a concomitant delicacy, an element of weight was needed. There are two statements of his which may be quoted to underpin this view. The first is from "How To Read" (1931). He is speaking of translations from Greek, and of Swinburne's particularly:

> The Greeks stimulated Swinburne; if he had defects, let us remember that, apart from Homer, the Greeks often

were rather Swinburnian. Catullus wasn't, or was but seldom. From which one may learn the nature of the Latin, non-Greek contribution to the art of expression.

At the conclusion of which it is only fair to say that he adds the footnote: "To be measured against the Sophoklean economy." The second is from "Notes on Elizabethan Classicists" (1918):

> . . . and the Greeks might be hard put to it to find a better poet among themselves than is their disciple Catullus. Is not Sappho, in comparison, a little, just a little Swinburnian?
>
> I do not state this as dogma, but one should be open to speculation.

It is true that the actual verbal structure of Greek does tend toward the allusive. The acme of finality is to be found in Roman rather than Greek epigram. There you have hardness and weight together. It was, I believe, when he read the half-dozen poems of T. E. Hulme that he realized the specific use to which he might be able to put his college studies of Martial and Catullus; for at both Pennsylvania and Hamilton, Horace, Martial and Catullus had been the three Roman poets to whom he had devoted most attention and for whom he had acquired a lifelong affection. I am told that Horace is quoted more frequently than any other Roman poet in the Cantos. I do not know how true this is. The influence of Martial is not as apparent as that of Catullus, but it is certainly present. While as for Catullus himself there is another passage from "How To Read" in which he tells us the exact poem which he would like to be able to emulate:

> In Rimbaud the image stands clean, unencumbered by non-functioning words; to get anything like this directness of presentation we must go back to Catullus, perhaps to the poem which contains *dentes habet*.

In a word, he hoped to write English poems technically comparable to Nos. 37 and 39 of the *Carmina*.

It is not easy for us at this length of time to recapture the full revolutionary flavor of such a notion. It meant discarding a great deal of what for more than a century had been considered the *sine qua non* of poetry. Even T. S. Eliot averred that his own tastes were "possibly too romantic" to appreciate Pound's epigrams to the full. The following is an extract from his Introduction to Pound's *Selected Poems*:

> [There is] a class of Pound's poems which may be called the Epigrams. These occur *passim* throughout Lustra. . . . There is, of course, acquaintance with Martial as well as with the epigrammatists of the Greek Anthology. . . . The reader must not be hasty in deciding whether Pound's epigrams 'come off'; for he should first examine his own soul whether he is capable of enjoying the very best epigram as poetry. (Mackail's Selections from the Greek Anthology are admirable except for being selections: that is, they tend to suppress the element of wit, the element of epigram, in the anthologists.) The reader who does not like Pound's epigrams should make very sure that he is not comparing them with the *Ode to a Nightingale* before he condemns them.

Eliot's comments are confirmed by the editors of the works of two of Pound's most successful precursors in the same field: Ben Jonson and Landor. Herford and Simpson, in their elaborate eleven-volume recension of Jonson's text, are loath to allow the title "poetry" to any of the Epigrams; while in Charles Crump's ten-volume Landor, the half-volume devoted to an unsatisfactory selection of the shorter poems is carefully headed "Poems and Epigrams."

In my experience, I am not alone in being unable to regard the productions of those years, 1910-30, in anything remotely resembling a "neo-classical" light—whatever the protestations of the artists themselves. This applies particularly to the high-spirited, delicate, touching poems of which *Personae* is so full. Nevertheless it is instructive to realize that in the first full-length study of Catullus to appear in English for twenty or thirty years, Professor Quinn, of Melbourne University,[1] although making considerable play

---

[1] *The Catullan Revolution* (Melbourne: Melbourne University Press, 1959).

Dedication of Canzoni, *1911.*

TO
OLIVIA AND DOROTHY SHAKESPEAR

First page of "Redondillas," an unpublished poem of 114 lines deleted from Canzoni. The page proofs, now in the Humanities Research Center at the University of Texas, show that Pound first tried to revise the poem before deleting it altogether.

> London is a woeful place,
> Shropshire is much pleasanter.
> Then let us smile a little space
> Upon fond nature's morbid grace.
>   *Oh, Woe, woe, woe, etcetera....*

Redondillas, or something of that sort [1]

I SING the gaudy to-day and cosmopolite civilization
  Of my hatred of crudities, of my weariness of banalities,
I sing of the ways that I love, of Beauty and delicate savours.

No man may pass beyond
    the nets of good and evil
For joy 's in deepest hell
    and in high heaven,.
About the very ports
    are subtle devils.

I would sing of exquisite sights
    of the murmur of Garda;
I would sing of the amber lights,
    or of how Desenzano
Lies like a topaz chain
    upon the throat of the waters.

I sing of natural forces
    I sing of refinements
I would write of the various moods
    of nuances, of subtleties.

Fifty years ago one would have called this effusion "The Age.

with aesthetic criteria such as would be acceptable in a literary common room (even going so far as to quote poems by W. H. Auden and Robert Graves), is still capable of citing poem 39 as one of Catullus' failures. The Professor quotes the first eight lines, translates them and concludes: "Here the attempt to transform prose statement by the structural force of repetition (e.g., the *renidet ille,* repeated at the same position in the line, the parallel *cum* clauses) somehow fails." But the quality of which Pound is speaking when he refers to this poem is not dependent on a simple matter of repetition. In the inability to grasp that intensive use of language which raises otherwise indifferent matter to the level of poetry we are back with Messrs. Crump, Herford and Simpson, *circa* 1910.

There is a poem by e. e. cummings which Pound quotes in his pamphlet *A Visiting Card* as an example of "Catullian ferocity." I do not know of any other poem by cummings that achieves quite the same effect. There is considerably more to Catullus than this, but it is the element that drives dynamically not only through poems 37 and 39, but others, such as 33, 57, 97 and those of the Gellius sequence.

>   flotsam and jetsam
>   are gentlemen poeds
>   urseappeal netsam
>   our spinsters and coeds)
>
>   thoroughly bretish
>   they scout the inhuman
>   itarian fetish
>   that man isn't wuman
>
>   vive the millenni
>   um three cheers for labor
>   give all things to enni
>   one buggar thy nabor
>
>   (neck and senecktie
>   are gentlemen ppoyds
>   even whose rectie
>   are covered by lloyds

The only poem in *Personae* in which Pound approaches the same savageness is "Salutation the Third." But it is altogether looser, with little or nothing of the Catullan qualities of sparseness and immediacy that he achieves elsewhere. The vitriol in Catullus is something he has never captured —or seriously sought to capture—for he is not temperamentally an angry writer. The contemplation of *dentes habet* and what he terms "the Latin, non-Greek contribution to the art of expression" helped him to write not so much Roman epigrams as Greek ones without a trace of Swinburnianism, or the sentimentality that plagued Landor when he made adaptations or translations from Greek. This last observation seems worth making because Landor, although a lesser poet, struck the Roman note of *gravitas* and finality in epigram more frquently than anyone in English other than Ben Jonson. Yet when he turned from the Romans to the Greeks he failed, and Pound—as I shall show—was quick to spot this.

Perhaps at this stage something should be said on the nature of the epigram in general, and those of Martial and Catullus in particular. When Martial proclaimed himself the conscious imitator of Catullus he was referring to the Catullus of the epigrams,[2] which are not the best part of his work. An epigram was originally something to be inscribed, or cut in stone. Hence the term "lapidary." It had to be brief, concise, pointed, the "point" occurring preferably in the last line or phrase. The final section (Nos. 69-116) or Catullus' volume is devoted to poems that fall very roughly into this category. They are all written in elegiacs, a meter common to epigram but by no means essential to it. (No. 76 is in the form of a love elegy, not an epigram, and the same term should probably be applied to No. 95.) In the first part of the book (Nos. 1-60) there are no elegiacs. A wide variety of lyric measures is used, some for the first, or almost the first, time in Roman poetry. Here too the resulting poem is often epigrammatic. The distinction between epigram and lyric, when the lyric had ceased to be a sung form, is not always easy to make. Poems such as 47, 53 and 59 are undoubtedly epigrammatic. They find their

[2] There is of course a certain formal resemblance in Martial's analogous use of hendecasyllables, but I am not referring to this.

equivalent in Pound in poems like "Phyllidula," "Quies," "Society," "The Three Poets" and the various items included under the head "Moeurs Contemporaines." For the reader's ease of reference I quote "Carmen 53,"

> Risi nescio quem modo e corona,
> qui, cum mirifice Vatiniana
> meus crimina Caluos explicasset,
> admirans ait haec manusque tollens,
> 'di magni, salaputium disertum!'

and "Soirée,"

> Upon learning that the mother wrote verses,
> And that the father wrote verses,
> And that the youngest son was in a publisher's
>   office,
> And that the friend of the second daughter was
>   undergoing a novel,
> The young American pilgrim
> Exclaimed:
>   "This is a darn'd clever bunch!"

Excellent though these, and other pieces like them, are, none represents the most developed, or individual, quality in either Catullus or Pound. For this, in Catullus, we have to turn to a poem such as 38, one of the three in the *Carmina* that Macaulay used to say he could never read without being moved to tears. (The other two were 8 and 76.)

> Malest, Cornifici, tuo Catullo,
> malest, me hercule, et laboriose,
> et magis magis in dies et horas.
> quem tu, quod minimum facillimumque est,
> qua solatus es allocutione?
> irascor tibi. sic meos amores?
> paulum quid lubet allocutionis,
> maestius lacrimis Simonideis.

The tone here is allusive and Greek. The thought "carries on" at the end, rather as in the *hokku* technique with which, as is well known, Pound also experimented in *Personae*. I think one is still bound to call such a poem an epigram, though very much in the Greek, rather than the Roman, manner. The following poem, "Carmen 46," I should prefer to call a lyric:

> Iam uer egelidos refert tepores,
> iam caeli furor aequinoctialis
> iucundis Zephyri silescit aureis.
> linquantur Phrygii, Catulle, campi
> Nicaeaque ager uber aestuosae:
> ad claras Asiae uolemus urbes.
> iam mens praetrepidans auet uagari,
> iam laeti studio pedes uigescunt.
> o dulces comitum ualete coetus,
> longe quos simul a domo profectos
> diuersae uarie uiae reportant.

These are the sort of poems whose echo occurs most frequently in Pound's work. The *gravitas* inherent in Martial, which makes him the first of all epigrammatists, is lacking in Catullus. Even his celebrated "Multas per gentes," which has both weight and finality, lacks the necessary tightness of syntax to make it a perfect epigram. (Which, I hasten to make clear, is not to say that it does not achieve its own perfection, which is of another order.) It may be worth quoting two short, but typical, examples from Martial to support my point. Here is No. 32 from Book IV of the Epigrams:

> Et latet et lucet Phaethontide condita gutta,
>   ut videatur apis nectare clusa suo.
>   dignum tantorum pretium tulit illa laborum:
>   credibile est ipsam sic voluisse mori.

and No. 44, from the same Book:

> Hic est pampineis viridis modo Vesbius umbris;
>   presserat hic madidos nobilis uva lacus;
> haec iuga, quam Nysae colles plus Bacchus amavit;
>   hoc nuper Satyri monte dedere choros;
> haec Veneris sedes, Lacedaemone gratior illi;
>   hic locus Herculeo numine clarus erat.
> cuncta iacent flammis et tristi mersa favilla:
>   nec superi vellent hoc licuisse sibi.

In contrast to Martial, however, with Catullus one thinks most readily of qualities such as "mischievousness," almost "naughtiness," rather than those of *gravitas* or moral seriousness. There is the vitriol, which we have already mentioned; and there is the pure lyricism. Besides this, there is a large element of what can most aptly be described as a spirit of *boulevarderie,* and this is a term that can also be applied to many of Pound's shorter pieces. He is never more Catullan than in all those gay, inconsequential poems in which he addresses his own work. Although so very different in subject, I find *The Study in Aesthetics* singularly reminiscent of No. 42 of the *Carmina,* while the two poems I should choose to place beside Nos. 38 and 46, which I have quoted above, are "The Garret":

> Come, let us pity those who are better off
> > than we are.
> Come, my friend, and remember
> > that the rich have butlers and no friends,
> And we have friends and no butlers.
> Come, let us pity the married and the unmarried.
>
> Dawn enters with little feet
> > like a gilded Pavlova,
> And I am near my desire.
> Nor has life in it aught better
> Than this hour of clear coolness,
> > the hour of waking together.

and "The Gypsy":

> That was the top of the walk, when he said:
> "Have you seen any others, any of our lot,
> "With apes or bears?"
> > —A brown upstanding fellow
> Not like the half-castes,
> > up on the wet road near Clermont.
> The wind came, and the rain,
> And mist clotted about the trees in the valley,
> And I'd the long ways behind me,
> > gray Arles and Biaucaire,
> And he said, "Have you seen any of our lot?"
>
> I'd seen a lot of his lot . . .
> > ever since Rhodez,
> Coming down from the fair
> > of St. John,
> With caravans, but never an ape or a bear.

Both the Latin and the English achieve that curious blend

of the direct and the allusive which it seems to me are among Catullus' and Pound's most distinctive attributes. The epigram, as a mode, shows how the temperaments of the two poets tend invariably toward the lyrical. Nor do I regard it as an accident that the two most deeply felt allusions to, or adaptations of, Catullus in the Cantos should be those in which the Greek element predominates. Poems 51 and 61 are taken as points of departure for an image, not of Catullus and Rome, but of Sappho and the early Greek world.

For fear that I should be thought to have dismissed too lightly Eliot's observations on Pound's epigrams, I append an example from Ben Jonson, than whom no one in the whole of English literature has imitated Martial more successfully, and a couple from Walter Savage Landor, whose strength, though slighter, lay in the same direction. Here is the Jonson:

"On Gut"
Gut eats all day, and letchers all the night,
   So all his meat he tasteth over, twice:
And striving so to double his delight,
   He makes himself a thorough-fare of vice.
Thus, in his belly, can he change a sin,
   Lust it comes out, that gluttony went in.

and here are the two from Landor:

Thy skin is like an unwashed carrot's,
Thy tongue is blacker than a parrot's,
Thy teeth are crooked but belong
Inherently to such a tongue.

"The Four Georges"
George the First was always reckoned
Vile but viler George the Second,
And what mortal ever heard
Any good of George the Third?
When from earth the Fourth descended
God be praised the Georges ended.

The distinction between these and the foregoing epigrams of Pound and Catullus should be plain enough. It is curious, however, that, as we have already observed, when Landor came to handle Greek matter, his astringency deserted him. In his copy of Landor, Pound has marked two of the five stanzas from "Pericles and Aspasia," which begin "Tanagra! think not I forget . . ." in such a way as to draw attention to unusually otiose or Miltonic elements. I quote stanzas 1 and 4 because the two men were, at least for part of their careers, bent on much the same task, that is, the resuscitation of the epigrammatic tradition, and also because of the special regard in which, in this context, Landor has always been held by Pound.

> Tanagra! think not I forget
>   Thy ~~beautifully~~ storied streets;
> Be sure my memory bathes yet
>   In clear Thermodon, and yet greets
> The (blithe and liberal) shepherd boy,
> (Whose sunny bosom swells with joy
> (When we accept his matted rushes
> Upheav'd with sylvan fruit; away he bounds, and blushes.)
>
> . . . .
>
> Sweetly where cavern'd Dirce flows
>   (Do) white-arm'd maidens chaunt my (lay,)
> Flapping (the while) with laurel-rose
>   The honey-gathering tribes away;
> And sweetly, sweetly Attic tongues
>   Lisp your Corinna's early songs;
> To her with feet more graceful (come)
> The verses that have dwelt in kindred breasts at home.

Somewhere, G. K. Chesterton has a remark about lightness of touch (which at the same time has point) bespeaking latent strength. It is presumably beause Pound and Jonson share great reserves of poetic purpose—not, of course, of the same sort—while Landor was only by accident a poet, that he could fall so short so frequently of his own canons, whereas the others almost never do of theirs. Consistency of achievement, at whatever level they are engaged, could be described as one of their more "classical" characteristics.

"Cloudy Riva," "Sapphire Benacus," together with various "sapphire tides," etc., a title "Phasellus Ille" and a dedication to Bridget Patmore, which in fact is the first line of Catullus' own, are not much as a basis on which to assert, as I have done, the depths of Catullus' influence on Ezra Pound. There are three translations, and a half-dozen references in the Cantos. And yet Garda is one of the places to which he has constantly returned, physically as well as mentally, or from which, in a sense, it would be fair to say that he has never been long absent. Catullus has helped him to write the most beautiful Greek epigrams—or epigrams tending toward lyrics—which there are in English. He admired the vitriol, but left it, wisely, on one side. He understood what Martial had done (no mean feat at that time); but, like Catullus, he is basically a lyric poet. "Doctrina" and "venustas," the two Catullan touchstones of "taste" and "elegance," are his also. More than any other of the great moderns, he would, one feels, have been at home with those "new poets"; he has displayed a similar impatience, irreverence, brilliance and integrity. And the goals have been identical:

> Even in my dreams you have denied yourself to me
> And sent me only your handmaids.

That is the note of Catullus and his circle, of the so-called "neoterics," of whom Cicero, apparently, thought so little.

As I sit typing this last paragraph I have beside me three of Dorothy Pound's imaginative watercolors of Garda and Sirmione. In two of them the waters are violet, with a touch of green in one; but in the third they are—I am glad to say—unmistakably sapphire. The dates on the back indicate the years 1910 and 1922. They have been constantly by me during the last few months, in which I have been completing my own work on Catullus[2]—a reminder that but for Pound's unremitting work, skill and extraordinary gifts of poetic insight I should not now have the weapons to do whatever it is I have done with Catullus. On more than one occasion, the pictures have sent me back to the *Pisan Cantos*, where there is a characteristic account of the first meeting between Joyce and Pound, which took place at Desenzano in the early twenties.

[2] Translation of the complete poems, for the Penguin Classics, to be published next year.—*Ed.*

> In fact a small rain storm . . .
>> as it were a mouse, out of cloud's mountain
> recalling the arrival of Joyce et fils
>> at the haunt of Catullus
> with Jim's veneration of thunder and the
>> Gardasee in magnificence
> But Miss Norton's memory for the conversation
>> (or 'go on') of idiots
> was such as even the eminent Irish writer
>> has, if equalled at moments (?synthetic'ly)
>> certainly never surpassed.

They might, of course, have met anywhere: they happened to meet on the shores of Garda; and at least one of the two had more than his share—a positively Catullan proportion—of literary vitriol in his character. It is not, however, with a memory of Joyce that I wish to end this piece, but with an evocation of Sirmione and of Catullus from a poet whose ear, at his rare best, was almost as fine as Pound's. It is amusing to recall that (however ironically) an alternative title pencilled in on the page proofs of one of the cancelled "Canzoni" was "Locksley Hall, or Fourty Years After"—a first try-out at a long poem. But whereas "Locksley Hall" remains one of the saddest monuments to Tennyson's largely wasted genius, his "Frater Ave atque Vale" is as fresh and arresting as the day it was written. In spite of the tourists, Sirmione and the lake and the olive trees among the ruins are still a little as he evokes them, and as Ezra Pound himself must first have seen them.

> Row us out from Desenzano, to your Sirmione row!
> So they row'd and there we landed—'O venusta Sirmio!'
> There to me thro' all the groves of olive in the summer
>> glow,
> There beneath the Roman ruin where the purple flowers
>> grow,
> Came that 'Ave atque Vale' of the Poet's hopeless woe,
> Tenderest of Roman poets nineteen hundred years ago,
> 'Frater Ave atque Vale'—as we wander'd to and fro
>> Gazing at the Lydian laughter of the Garda Lake below
>> Sweet Catullus's all-but-island, olive-silvery Sirmio!

Like Catullus and Pound, he was a dab-hand at *nugae*—if only he had known it.

THE SEARCH FOR MRS. WOOD'S PROGRAM

by Donald Gallup

I FIRST HEARD of Mrs. Wood's concert program in 1956. In going over the carbon copies at Yale of some of Ezra Pound's letters, I came across two references:

> Mrs. Wood wants me to translate some french & Italian songs for her concert program & as I only have till dinner time to do five mss, perhaps I'd better attend to it. *(E.P. to his mother, February 19, 1910)*

> I send along Mrs. Wood's concert program. The translations are not particularly valuable, having been scribbled off, the lot of them, in one day. All but the first Verlaine, which I had done, more or less, some time ago. *(E.P. to his father, March 2, 1910)*

There didn't seem to be much point even in looking for a copy of this item in the United States, and I filed the references away among problems for investigation in Italy and England during the following summer.

But in June, 1957, at Rapallo, Olga Rudge and I could find no trace of the program among the printed material then in her custody; and later, at Brunnenburg, Mary de Rachewiltz was not able to locate the early scrapbooks kept by Homer Pound, in which the copy E.P. had sent home in 1910 might well have been placed. A few weeks later, in

Mrs. Wood's program.

BECHSTEIN HALL.

TUESDAY, MAR. 1st, at 8.15

Miss FLORENCE
SCHMIDT
and Miss ELSIE
HALL

Vocal and Pianoforte Recital

Accompanist: Miss DAISY BUCKTROUT

BECHSTEIN GRAND PIANOFORTE.

BOOK OF WORDS · · SIXPENCE

London, I had no better luck, but Agnes Bedford—who arranged the music for E.P.'s *Five Troubadour Songs* (1920) and selected the passages from William Atheling for *Antheil and the Treatise on Harmony* (1924)—very kindly interested herself in the search. After I had returned to the United States, she reported to me that she had discovered that Mrs. Wood was still alive and residing in North Cornwall. I wrote her and received this reply:

> Dear Mr. Gallup, Your letter was a strange reminder of the past. Memories of poor Ezra Pound. I well remember the translations he kindly did for me of the French-Italian words of my recital programme. Alas! two World Wars have sadly disrupted my life & possessions & I no longer have them. It is strange to recall those days when Ezra would "intone" his poems to us of an evening. I fear we used to think his recital of them somewhat unusual if not eccentric & we little thought then that his works would be held in such esteem in future years. He gave me a copy of his first book of poems with an inscription that also I no longer possess. It must have been about 1912 [1910?] when he brought D. H. Lawrence to our house. We were always "at home" on a Saturday evening to friends & their friends & one of these [evenings] Ezra was dining with us & near the end of dinner he mentioned he had asked a friend to come in a school teacher from Croydon called Lawrence. Hardly had he said so when the maid ushered in a strange man & in greeting him I asked casually if he had had dinner & he said No. My maid then brought him in the previous courses & we continued with the meal. He certainly was not at all prepossessing looking—a scruffy moustache & unruly hair. During the evening he sat on a stool at my feet & positively charmed me & I fear I neglected my other guests. Next day he wrote me a delightful letter saying how much he had enjoyed himself. This was of course before he had any of his books published. I never saw him again but had another letter regretting he could not come to my recital as he was ill in bed with a bad cold & was watching the window blind cord tap endlessly on the pane. Forgive these reminiscences—a sign of old age—but your letter has conjured up such memories. So sorry I cannot help you.
>
> Yrs sincerely
> Florence Derwent Wood.

Mrs. Wood and I exchanged other letters, and in December she wrote that she had heard from her old accompanist, who thought that she might find the program among her records and would look for it. "If successful I will send you the results." But if the search was made, it was apparently not successful, for I heard nothing more. Agnes Bedford wrote E.P. himself but, although he remembered the occasion, he had no idea as to where a copy of the program might be found. And there the matter rested, more or less, for three years.

In August, 1961, just before I left the United States for England, I wrote again to Mrs. Wood. It had occurred to me that she might possibly remember the name of the printer of the program and, if the firm still existed, I might be able to see their file copy. But she answered—not at all surprisingly after fifty years—that she could not recall the name. She had as a last resort written once again to her old accompanist, but the answer was discouraging. She enclosed the first two pages of the reply, which explained that, although the program might well be in a cabin trunk in her kitchen, the trunk was buried under suitcases and boxes, and she could not possibly pull it out since her arthritis made it impossible for her to bend; in short, she could do nothing.

But here was at least some hope that a copy of the program did actually exist. I had received Mrs. Wood's letter in London and, although I did not at the time know the name of the accompanist, her address appeared at the head of her letter: 35 Holbein House, S. W. 1; I promptly took a bus to Knightsbridge. Holbein House is a large apartment building and 35 turned out to be on the sixth floor. There was no lift, but I soon arrived before the door, breathless from exercise and anticipation, and knocked. After a long pause, I heard footsteps accompanied by the tap of a cane and the door was opened by an old, well-preserved lady of somewhat forbidding mien, wearing a large hat trimmed with feathers. Not knowing her name, I could only wave Mrs. Wood's letter by way of introduction, as I tried to convey the importance to me of the program and to offer my help in pulling out the trunk for her so that she could examine its contents. Yes, Mrs. Wood had written her, but no, it was quite impossible for her to look for the program, and equally impossible for me to be of any assistance. Besides, the songs in the program had only been translated by Mr. Pound and they could hardly be of any importance to anyone. In any case, she repeated, it was quite impossible for her to do anything to help me. There was nothing for me to do but smile wanly and amble dejectedly back down all those stairs.

I told my sad story to Agnes Bedford when I saw her the next afternoon, and she agreed to do what she could to find some friend of Daisy Bucktrout's—for Daisy Bucktrout was indeed the accompanist's name—who might intercede with her on my behalf. A few days afterward, she wrote me saying that the friend she had approached didn't feel that she knew Miss Bucktrout well enough to interfere.

In desperation, just before leaving London for a few days in Cambridge, I wrote Miss Bucktrout a letter, explaining again how important the program was to me, once more volunteering to haul out the trunk, depart, and return whenever she wished me to, to put everything back in order. As if in afterthought, I added that I would gladly pay for the program if a copy were found. I enclosed a stamped self-addressed envelope for her reply. When I returned from Cambridge, the envelope was awaiting me at my hotel. But the letter it contained merely reiterated that Miss Bucktrout could not under any circumstances help me in my search.

I had not really allowed myself to put much hope in the faint possibility of persuading Daisy Bucktrout to relent and had written another letter to Mrs. Wood in Cornwall, asking her where the recital had been given. I had a prompt reply: She had sung at the Bechstein Hall on Wigmore Street, under her maiden name, Florence Schmidt. Now the obvious question was, what had become of Bechstein Hall? It was certainly not listed in the telephone book and the piano-manufacturing firm equally seemed not to be listed in London. After numerous inquiries, I appealed once more to Agnes Bedford. When I telephoned her, she was not surprised to hear that Mrs. Wood had sung as Florence Schmidt, for she herself had discovered this in 1957, although she had not mentioned it to me. She was able to tell me at once that Bechstein Hall had during World War I been rechristened Wigmore Hall. This was excellent news, for even I knew that Wigmore Hall still existed. Miss Bedford added that the present manager had been connected with the Hall for many years, and thought it quite likely that the Hall would have at least some old programs.

I passed an almost sleepless night and with difficulty restrained myself from going to Wigmore Street before I could be reasonably sure that the manager would be there. But at last the time arrived. The ticket sellers at the box office were hardly optimistic about my chances, but did grudgingly consent to call the manager. I explained to him briefly what it was I wanted. "But, my dear fellow," he replied, "do you realize how many programs we would have if we kept them all? We'd need a separate storehouse!" I admitted that this was indeed true, but ventured even so to hope that some of the early ones might have been kept in more leisurely, roomier days. At last he agreed to see what he could do, promising nothing, and I began to write out the details to leave with him.

As I wrote he seemed to go into a kind of trance. Almost as if to himself he chanted slowly: "Now let me see, don't I remember some old volumes downstairs somewhere—?" This had me on the edge of my seat. "Yes? Yes?" I cried excitedly. "Come along," he said. "Mind you, I'm not promising anything, and I warn you it'll be dusty work, but we'll see what we can find."

I followed him down the stairs to the basement of the Hall and we came to a small room where a man was at work mounting posters. There against the far wall were three shelves, their contents hidden by curtains. The manager lifted the top curtain to reveal a row of perhaps ten to fifteen folio volumes uniformly bound in a kind of buckram. Excitedly I examined the dates taped on their spines; alas! they were mostly of the thirties. But I had already grasped at the curtain hanging below; here the stamped dates were of the twenties. I dropped to my knees and pulled at the curtain covering the remaining, lowest row: here were 1912-13, 1911-12, 1910-11 and, at last, 1909-10! I seized the volume, pulled it out, and placed it unceremoniously on the floor. "There's probably an index," the manager said, "why don't you look there?" But, knowing the approximate date, I had already turned to that section. Sure enough, a flier announced the joint recital of Florence Schmidt and Elsie Hall on Tuesday, March 1. And there, underneath, was the actual program, securely pasted in. A glance revealed that two of the English texts were signed Ezra Pound, and I knew that I had found what I was looking for. I jumped up and clapped the manager on the shoulder, and he seemed himself to have caught some of my excitement.

Now came the problem of how I was to copy the document, for it contained seven printed quarto pages.[1] The manager and I lifted the volume to a table and he, to my astonishment, began to tear the program from the sheet of heavier paper to which its last leaf was fastened. I protested, and without much trouble accomplished its removal with-

[1] A group each of Italian, French and English, and a second group of French songs, as sung by Miss Schmidt, with English versions of the Italian and French songs by Ezra Pound. (These are separated by three groups of titles of "Pianoforte Soli" performed by Miss Hall.) Except for the "Chanson Provençal" in the final group, of which only the English version is printed, texts appear in a left-hand column, with English versions at right. Only the English versions of the first two French songs have printed attribution to Ezra Pound. The Italian and French groups are as follows:

Aria:	(a) Cantata Spirituale	Leonardo Leo
Siciliana:	(b) "Tre giorni son che Nina"	Pergolesi
Aria:	(c) "Non so più cosa son" *(Le Nozze di Figaro)*	Mozart
Songs:	(a) Clair de Lune [text by Paul Verlaine]	Gabriel Fauré
	(b) Lied Maritime [text by the composer]	Vincent d'Indy
	(c) "Ariettes Oubliées (No. 3) [text by Verlaine]	Debussy
	(d) "Aquarelles" (Green) [text by Verlaine]	Debussy
	(e) "Fêtes Galantes"—Fantoches [text by Verlaine]	Debussy
Songs:	(a) "Lisette" (Bergerette) [Old French text]	XVIII. Century
	(b) Chanson Provençal	
Aria:	(c) "Manon"	Massenet

out damage to the pamphlet itself. To my further amazement the manager agreed to let me take it away to be photographed on my promise to have it back that afternoon. I thanked him profusely and walked out of Wigmore Hall treading the red carpets very lightly indeed.

Now the Times Book Club is next door to Wigmore Hall and only a few days earlier I had purchased a few books there, having them sent to New Haven. When I gave my name, the assistant said, "Oh, Mr. Eliot's bibliographer?" and I, very much flattered, acknowledged the identification. It occurred to me that possibly this agreeable young man (whom I later identified as Timothy d'Arch Smith) might know where I could have photographs of the program made on short order, and I stopped to ask him. It turned out that there was a duplicating machine in the shop and in a matter of minutes I had some very good copies of the seven printed pages. Waving them in one hand, and with the original program clutched in the other, I returned to Wigmore Hall and handed the program to the somewhat astonished manager. I offered to paste it back into the proper volume, but he insisted upon doing this himself. All I could do was take his name: H. T. C Brickell, Manager, Wigmore Hall; promise to acknowledge my indebtedness to him; and thank him again for his kindness.

Thus, on my last day in London before leaving for France and Italy, September 27, 1961, the search for Mrs. Wood's concert program came to a happy end.

EZRA POUND AND THE BOLLINGEN PRIZE

by Allen Tate

WHAT I SHALL say here is not in further commentary on Mr. William Barrett's article in the April, 1949, issue of *Partisan Review;* nor is it the "rational, impersonal, and calm justfication" of the award of the Bollingen Prize to Ezra Pound which Mr. Barrett was kind enough to expect from me. I intend rather to set down my own reasons for voting for the *Pisan Cantos.* I shall have in mind the *Partisan* symposium on the award without, I hope, being influenced by it in reconstructing my views of last November.[1]

From the time I first read Pound's verse more than thirty years ago I have considered him a mixed poet. In an essay written in 1931, on the first thirty Cantos, I expressed views which the later accretions to the work have not changed: the work to which I helped to give the Bollingen Prize is formless, eccentric and personal. The Cantos are now, as I said then, "about nothing at all." They have a voice but

[1] The first award of the Bollingen Prize was made in 1949 to Ezra Pound for the *Pisan Cantos,* published in 1948; but the prize was voted to him in November, 1948, by the Fellows in American Letters of the Library of Congress, who were then the jury of the award. I was a member of the jury. Since 1950 the Bollingen Prize has been under the auspices of the Yale University Library.

no subject. As one of the commentators on Mr. Barrett's article put it, they have no beginning, middle or end. I used similar language in 1931. It is a striking fact that in talking about this work one must say "Canto XX of the Cantos"; there is always a Canto of Cantos, not a Canto of a substantive work with a title like "Canto XX" of the *Purgatorio* of the *Divina Commedia*.

Mr. Pound is incapable of sustained thought in either prose or verse. His acute verbal sensibility is thus at the mercy of random flights of "angelic insight," Icarian self-indulgences of prejudice which are not checked by a total view to which they could be subordinated. Thus his anti-Semitism—which, as Mr. Auden has said, all Gentiles have felt (I have felt it, and felt humiliated by it)—his anti-Semitism is not disciplined by an awareness of its sinister implications in the real world of men. Neither Mr. Pound nor any other man is to be censured for his private feelings; but every man must answer for what he does with his feelings. It has been often observed that Pound fails to get into his verse any sort of full concrete reality. Insofar as the Cantos have a subject, it is made up of historical materials. But if there is any poetry of our age which may be said to be totally lacking in the historical sense, the sense of how ideas move in history, it is Pound's Cantos. His verse is an anomaly in an age of acute historical awareness.

I do not know what reasons, motives or prejudices prompted the other affirmative votes. There has been some public conjecture upon this subject, but I consider it a gross impropriety. I shall do well if I am able to speak honestly for myself. I have little sympathy with the view that holds that Pound's irresponsible opinions merely lie alongside the poetry, which thus remains uncontaminated. The disagreeable opinions are right in the middle of the poetry. And they have got to be seen for what they are: they are personal, willful and unrelated; and they are not brought together under a mature conception of life as it is now or ever was. I infer the absence of such a mature view in the man from the incoherence of the form; but it is only the latter that concerns me. Apart from specific objections to his anti-Semitism and fascism, there is a formal principle which, if severely applied, would have been a good enough reason for voting against the *Pisan Cantos*. Not only the anti-Semitism but all the other "insights" remain unassimilated to a coherent form. The assumption of many persons that a vote for the *Pisan Cantos* was a vote for "formalism" and a vote against "vitality" in poetry makes no sense at all to me.

There is nothing mysterious about coherent form. It is the presence of an order in a literary work which permits us to understand one part in relation to all the other parts. What should concern us in looking *at* the Cantos is the formal irresponsibility; in looking *beyond* the work, the possible effects of this irresponsibility upon society. (If Pound's Cantos expressed *anti*-fascist opinions, my formal objections would be the same; but I should think that the formlessness would make him a good Communist party-line poet.) But just as Pound's broadcasts over Radio Rome never influenced anybody in this country, and were chiefly an indignity perpetrated upon himself, I cannot suppose that the anti-Semitism of the Cantos will be taken seriously by anybody but liberal intellectuals. Anti-Semites will not "use" it. It is too innocent. I take it seriously in the sense of disliking it, and I cannot "honor the man" for it, as the Fellows of the Library were charged with doing; but I cannot think that it will strengthen anti-Semitism.

I respect differences of opinion on this question, about which I am not well informed. What I have already said is enough to indicate that my vote for the *Pisan Cantos* was not an easy step to take; I could have voted against it. But this is not all. I had, as many men of my generation might have had, personal reasons for not voting for Mr. Pound. Insofar as he has noticed my writings at all, in conversation and correspondence—which the international literary grapevine always reports—he has noticed them with contempt.

Nevertheless I voted for him, for the following reason: the health of literature depends upon the health of society, and conversely; there must be constant vigilance for both ends of the process. The specific task of the man of letters is to attend to the health of society *not at large* but through literature—that is, he must be constantly aware of the condition of language in his age. As a result of observing Pound's use of language in the past thirty years I had become convinced that he had done more than any other man to regenerate the language, if not the imaginative forms, of English verse. I had to face the disagreeable fact that he had done this even in passages of verse in which the opinions expressed ranged from the childish to the detestable.

In literature as in life nothing reaches us pure. The task of the civilized intelligence is one of perpetual salvage. We cannot decide that our daily experience must be either aesthetic or practical—art of life; it is never, as it comes to us, either/or; it is always both/and. But as persons of a particular *ethos,* of a certain habit and character, we discharge our responsibilities to society from the point of view of the labors in which we are placed. We are placed in the profession of letters. We cannot expect the businessman and the politician, the men who run the state, to know that our particular responsibility exists; we cannot ask them to understand the more difficult fact that our responsibility to them is for the language which they themselves use for the general welfare. They are scarcely aware of language at all; what one is not aware of one almost inevitably abuses. But the medium cannot be extricated from the material, the how from the what; part of our responsibility is to correct the monism of the statesman who imagines that what he says is scarcely said in language at all, that it exists apart from the medium in a "purity" of action which he thinks of as "practicality." If men of letters do not look after the medium, nobody else will. We need never fear that the practical man will fail to ignore our concern for the health of language; this he has already done by indicting Pound as if Pound, like himself, were a monist of action. Pound's language remains our particular concern. If he were a convicted traitor, I should still think that, in another direction which complicates the problem ultimately beyond our comprehension, he had performed an indispensable duty to society.

THE RETURN OF THE LONG POEM

by Hugh MacDiarmid

Ezra Pound is undoubtedly the greatest living poet writing in any form of the English language. T. S. Eliot was right when he called him "il miglior fabbro." Where in the course of his output Eliot contracted, Pound has expanded. There is no need here to consider the way he has always been in the forefront of technical developments, or his seminal influence on other important writers, or the brilliance of his work as a translator (or adaptor, if you like—I am not concerned with pedantic considerations of the extent of his knowledge of the languages with which he has intromitted)—my interest concentrates on the major character of the first of all these aspects of his creative activity, namely, the Cantos. Many of those who are ready to recognize his importance in other respects jib when it comes to the Cantos, and find that in these all his other gifts have run irremediably into the sand. On the contrary I think it can be shown that they constitute the consummation and crowning of all the various powers exemplified in his previous writings.

For what is meant by great poet? What combination of qualities constitutes supreme poetic art? It has been said—and I accept the definition—that these qualities are three:

(1) robustness of thought; (2) felicity of expression; (3) comprehensiveness of view. Many poets possess all of these qualities in *large* measure, many more possess one or other of them in *full* measure, but exceedingly few possess all three in full measure. The purely lyric poet, by the very character of his muse, is incapable of excelling in the first quality—robustness of thought. English poetry today consists almost entirely of short lyrics. These are quite incapable of measuring up to the requirements of our age with its great scientific discoveries and unprecedented acceleration of change. The best of these lyric poets may be recommended to read the late Professor Laura Richthofer's *Heine,* in which she shows in the most convincing way how Heine, after the great success of his early lyrics, found he must cease to write in that way altogether and needed to break up the unity of the lyric, create a new form that would accommodate shifting tonalities and levels so that he could introduce, and grapple with, all manner of diverse subject matter and feelings. That crisis lasted for years before Heine solved his problem in his later work, which for that very reason has been either largely ignored or underestimated in comparison with the earlier lyrics he had found it necessary to abandon. It was obviously just as necessary for Pound to sheer away altogether from his earlier work with its *fin-de-siecle* characteristics and derivation from the nineties, and strike out in a different direction altogether. He did so, Heaven only knows at what cost—for such remaking of oneself is always a terrible undertaking—and plunged far ahead of the point at which Heine's difficulties found their resolution.

Writing of contemporary English poetry forty years ago, Mr. H. P. Collins said that he had gone scrupulously through the whole of a widely acclaimed volume of Georgian poetry, not without pleasure, and afterward reflected with consternation that never for an instant had he the sensation of being in contact with the serious creative intelligence of a great modern nation.

That only brought up to the time it was written just what Mathew Arnold said in the first *Essays on Criticism:*

It has long seemed to me that the burst of creative activity in our literature, through the first quarter of this century, had about it in fact something premature; and that from this cause its productions are doomed, most of them, in spite of our sanguine hopes which accompanied and do still accompany them, to prove hardly more lasting than the productions of far less splendid epochs. And this prematureness comes from its having proceeded without having its proper data, without sufficient material to work with. In other words, the English poetry of the first quarter of this century with plenty of energy, plenty of creative force, did not know enough. This makes Byron so empty of matter, Shelley so incoherent, Wordsworth even, profound as he is, yet so wanting in completeness and variety.

I do not think it can be contended that any subsequent poet in English, till we come to Eliot and Pound, has "known enough"; most English readers so far as poetry is concerned are still living on the kind of poetry, or some weaker derivative of it, Arnold was exposing as inadequate and transient. If that bad influence ever disappears Pound will have been the main cause.

"The sovereign poet," said Seeley, "must be not only a singer, but a sage; to passion and music he must add large ideas and abundant knowledge; he must extend in width as well as in height; but besides this he must be no dreamer or fanatic; he must be as firmly rooted in the hard earth as he spreads widely and mounts freely towards the sky."

The present writer has said elsewhere,

The poetry of the past can only be properly appreciated when it is seen in its proper historical setting. The whole position of poetry has been menaced by the insistence in schools and elsewhere on the poetry of the past, divorced from vital current interests, which is as if children were compelled to learn Sanskrit or Anglo-Saxon before they learned English; and by our insistence that the general public must have things made as simple as possible for them. This, to my mind, is simply not true, and only a 'superior' bourgeois assumption, flattering to themselves and convenient to their interests as lecturers, teachers, reviewers, journalists and so forth. There is no divergence between the interests of the masses and the real highbrows. On the contrary, what menaces the deepest interests of the masses is all that would 'keep them in their place,' spoon-feed them, pretend that certain things are beyond them and that they must be restricted to the conventional, the familiar, the easy. In the last resort, this makes for their stabilization—as the masses—in contradistinction to the classes; and finally it makes for the short-circuiting of consciousness, whereas all that is experimental, creative, repudiative of facile simplifications and established modes (incompatible, that is, with Pound's great slogan, "Make It New") moves in the opposite direction.

Ezra Pound shows in the Cantos that he has never allowed himself to be (in Sean O'Casey's phrase) drawn away from "the sensitive extension of the world." There are few poets of whom this can be said, and Pound towers head and shoulders over them all.

It is the complicated which seems to be Nature's climax of rightness. The simple is at a discount. Poetry has nothing to do with religious mysticism but is entirely an affair of the practical reason. Our mind is part and parcel of terrestrial Nature, in which it is immersed, and there and only there can it meet with requitals and fulfillments. We are living in a time of unprecedented and ever-accelerating change. The insistent demand everywhere is for higher and higher skills, and as automation increases this will intensify. Hence it is good to see that in his latest work Pound is on the plane of what Teilhard de Chardin calls the *noösphere*. Much has been written recently of the need to bridge the gulf between the arts and the sciences. The call is for synthesis. Stress is laid on the fact that we are living in a great quantitative rather than qualitative age and that the only form adequate to the classless society is the epic—not like epics of the past, except in scale, but embodying a knowledge of the modern world and all its potentialities, not in bits and pieces, but in the round.

The reason Eliot is so inferior to Pound is simply that he never realized (moved indeed always further away from the realization) that what poetry (English poetry especially) needs above all is to break out of confinement to a more earthly endaemonism with Christian nuances—that pseudo-religious mental climate which keeps our harmonies and solutions on so contemptibly shallower a level than the conflicts and tragedies which encompass our lives.

Most English readers are automatically alienated from Pound's later work by the absence of that pseudo-religiosity they have been taught is synonymous with poetry.

The opinion of most people has been so conditioned —that omnipresent brainwashing of our society so effective— that few people nourished on Palgrave's *Golden Treasury*, the English Association's *Poems of Today* and perhaps the several volumes of *Georgian Poetry* cannot believe it is true that, as D. G. James says in *Scepticism and Poetry:*

> When we consider the tradition of English poetry since the Reformation, it is obvious that it is not a Christian poetic tradition. None of the major poets, with the exception of Milton, have written as Christians. The case of Wordsworth is of enormous interest and importance to us. During the years of his greatest poetic output he wrote as a man of passionately religious imagination, but not as a Christian. After his acceptance of Christianity he wrote indeed much fine poetry, but the fact of a decline of his poetic power is undeniable. Keats and Shakespeare sought to evolve their own mythologies; Wordsworth satisfied his imagination in the contemplation of Christian dogma, which considered as a mythology is absolute, where those of Shakespeare and Keats are halting and inexpressive. . . . In Wordsworth, the non-Christian tradition in English poetry once more adopted Christianity; but to its detriment. Wordsworth's later poetry is therefore the most perfect comment we have upon the present state of the mind of our civilisation; for Wordsworth, who, when all is said and done, possessed one of the most powerful imaginations of our time, sought out Christianity and made it his own, only to impair, though by no means to destroy, the sources of his poetry. And we choose before the dogmatic poetry of the later Wordsworth the poetic failures of Keats and of Shakespeare.

Pound in the Cantos has led the way to the return of the

long poem and to the implementation of Mr. D. G. James's ungainsayable finding that

> as in science the formulation of a theorem must lead to further enquiry and research, so in poetry the enjoyment of poetic experience of any part of the world is fraught with the necessity of discovering a wider and more inclusive imaginative apprehension, in which more and more elements in experience are caught up and incorporated. The imagination of the great poet at least never rests from this momentous labour which endeavours to encompass the whole of life, and to achieve a comprehensive unity of imaginative pattern. In many minds, though by no means in all, such a labour, issuing in a failure to achieve such a harmony, leads on to an imaginative apprehension of life in which the world or our experience is seen as only fragmentary, and as a part of a wider reality which in its totality is susceptible only of the dimmest apprehension. Only in the light of that wider reality is this world seen as bodying forth a unity, a unity which in itself it does not possess. For some minds such an imagination of life comes to have a compulsive and controlling reality; an 'unknown and no more' takes on an overwhelming significance for the whole of life. The imagination in its passion for unity and harmony is driven to the indulgence of this 'dream', which, whether in reality it be 'dream' or not, is 'a presence which is not to be put by', and which conditions the whole of life. In other words, it is precisely the encompassment of the world by the imagination which is seen to be impossible; the essential labour of the imagination, its passion for unity and order, is defeated by experience; and whatsoever of unity and order life is seen to possess hangs on the sense of that which baffles the imagination. . . . As Mr. Eliot has said, religion is never wholly freed of scepticism; but it needs to be added, what is equally true, that scepticism can never wholly liberate itself from faith. Faith is 'somehow integrated' into scepticism, just as scepticism is 'somehow integrated' into faith. In these matters it is not given to us to *know*. The 'denial' into which some scepticism issues cannot be absolute. As Kant said, religion is an affair of the *practical* reason; and for this reason explicit assertion or denial is superficial in its implications. Thus, it is in effect impossible to draw

a line of division between what we call faith and what we call scepticism, for each is, whether it realises it or not, 'integrated' into the other. If this is so, the poetry of mysticism exhibits something latent in all imaginative apprehension of the world which seeks to be comprehensive.

Apart from T. S. Eliot's *Four Quartets* and Pound's Cantos we must look elsewhere than to English literature for the best examples of the return of the long poem. We are apt to think that the poetic production of the socialist countries is confined, on the one hand, to short poems on a simple folk song basis, or, on the other, commonplace pieces of propagandist doggerel. That is not the case.

The character of the times, the tremendous revolutions through which we are passing have enforced the realization that what is needed now are giant syntheses—not only in prose but also in poetry. Mayakovsky's poems *Vladimir Ilyitch Lenin* and *Harasho* (*The Poem of October*) render in an impressive and lyrical synthesis the history of the preparation and carrying out of the first socialist revolution in the world.

The Chilean Pablo Neruda celebrates the fight for national liberation waged by the peoples of Latin America in monumental cycles of poems, such as the well-known *Canto General* or the more recent *Cancion de gesta,* devoted to revolutionary Cuba—not unlike the huge mural frescoes painted by the Mexican painters.

The Turkish poet Nazim Hikmet worked out a colossal poetical edifice planned in nine volumes, with more than three thousand heroes, suggestively called *Human Panorama,* or *History of the Twentieth Century.* After the "epic" *The Desert and Spring* Vladimir Lugovski wrote, in fourteen years, the great work of his life, *The Middle of the Century,* a book of poems which he called *The Century's Autobiography,* the result of profound lyrical and philosophical meditations on man, mankind, happiness and politics.

These poems represent the growing end of poetry today, corresponding to the vast complexity of the modern world and the unparalleled perspectives opening out before man-

Title page of T. S. Eliot's anonymous Ezra Pound: His Metric and Poetry, *1917*.

EZRA POUND
HIS METRIC AND POETRY

Drawing of Ezra Pound by Henri Gaudier-Brzeska

NEW YORK · ALFRED A. KNOPF · 1917

Opening page of Ezra Pound: His Metric and Poetry.

EZRA POUND
HIS METRIC AND POETRY

I

"All talk on modern poetry, by people who know," wrote Mr. Carl Sandburg in *Poetry*, "ends with dragging in Ezra Pound somewhere. He may be named only to be cursed as wanton and mocker, poseur, trifler and vagrant. Or he may be classed as filling a niche today like that of Keats in a preceding epoch. The point is, he will be mentioned."

This is a simple statement of fact. But though Mr. Pound is well known, even having been the victim of interviews for Sunday papers, it does not follow that his work is thoroughly known. There are twenty people who have their opinion of him for every one who has read his writings with any care. Of those twenty, there will be some who are shocked, some who are ruffled, some who are irritated, and one or two whose sense of dignity is outraged. The twenty-first critic will probably be one who knows and admires some of the poems, but who either says: "Pound is primarily a scholar, a translator," or "Pound's early verse was beautiful; his later work shows nothing better than the itch for advertisement, a mischievous desire to be annoying, or a childish desire to be original." There is a third type of reader, rare enough,

The first Pound bibliography, compiled by Pound himself for Eliot's Ezra Pound: His Metric and Poetry.

BIBLIOGRAPHY
OF
BOOKS AND PARTIAL BIBLIOGRAPHY OF
NOTABLE CRITICAL ARTICLES
BY
EZRA POUND

POEMS

A LUME SPENTO (100 copies). Antonelli, Venice, June, 1908.
A QUINZAINE FOR THIS YULE.
    First 100 printed by Pollock, London, December, 1908.
    Second 100 published under Elkin Mathews' imprint, London, December, 1908.
PERSONÆ. Mathews, London, Spring, 1909.
EXULTATIONS. Mathews, London, Autumn, 1909.

PROSE

THE SPIRIT OF ROMANCE. Dent, London, 1910.

POEMS

PROVENÇA (a selection of poems from "Personæ" and "Exultations" with new poems). Small Maynard, Boston, 1910.
CANZONI. Mathews, London, 1911.
THE SONNETS AND BALLATE OF GUIDO CAVALCANTI (translated). Small Maynard, Boston, 1912.
    A cheaper edition of the same, Swift and Co., London, 1912.
        The bulk of this edition destroyed by fire.

29

RIPOSTES. Swift, London, 1912.
>   (*Note.*—This book contains the first announcement of Imagism, in the foreword to the poems of T. E. Hulme.)

OTHER PUBLICATIONS

"A FEW DON'TS BY AN IMAGISTE," in "Poetry," for March, 1913.
"CONTEMPORANIA" (poems), in "Poetry," April, 1913.

POEMS

PERSONÆ, EXULTATIONS, CANZONI, RIPOSTES, published in two volumes. Mathews, London, 1913.
FIRST OF THE NOTES ON JAMES JOYCE, "Egoist," January, 1914.
FIRST OF THE ARTICLES CONCERNING GAUDIER-BRZESKA, "Egoist," February, 1914.

OTHER PUBLICATIONS

"DES IMAGISTES," poems by several authors selected by Ezra Pound, published as a number of "The Glebe," in New York. February, 1914.
>   Alfred Kreymborg was at this time editor of "The Glebe." The first arrangements for the anthology were made through the kind offices of John Cournos during the winter of 1912-13.
>   The English edition of this anthology published by The Poetry Book Shop. London, 1914.

ARTICLE ON WYNDHAM LEWIS, "Egoist," June 15, 1914.
CONTRIBUTIONS TO FIRST NUMBER OF "Blast," June 20, 1914.
"VORTICISM," an article in "The Fortnightly Review," September, 1914.
"GAUDIER-BRZESKA," an article in "The New Age," February 4, 1915.
CONTRIBUTIONS to second number of "Blast," 1915.

30

POEMS

Cathay. Mathews, London, April, 1915. (Translations from the Chinese from the notes of Ernest Fenollosa.)

OTHER PUBLICATIONS

The Catholic Anthology, edited by Ezra Pound. Mathews, London, December, 1915.

Gaudier-Brzeska, a memoir. John Lane, London and New York, 1916.

Lustra (poems) public edition, pp. 116. Mathews, London, 1916.
200 copies privately printed and numbered, pp. 124.

Certain Noble Plays of Japan. Cuala Press, Dundrum, Ireland, 1916. Translated by Ernest Fenollosa and Ezra Pound, with an introduction by William Butler Yeats.

Noh, or Accomplishment. A study of the Classical Stage of Japan, including translations of fifteen plays, by Ernest Fenollosa and Ezra Pound. Macmillan, London, 1917. Knopf, New York, 1917.

Passages from the Letters of John Butler Yeats, selected by Ezra Pound, with brief editorial note. Cuala Press, 1917.

Lustra, with Earlier Poems, Knopf, New York, 1917. (This collection of Mr. Pound's poems contains all that he now thinks fit to republish.)
There is also a privately-printed edition of fifty copies, with a reproduction of a drawing of Ezra Pound by Henri Gaudier-Brzeska (New York, 1917).

Pavannes and Divisions (Prose), in preparation. Knopf, New York.

kind as a result of the tremendous developments of the sciences in our time. But by far the greatest of these is Pound's Cantos, since the others are comparatively plantigrade, lacking altogether "the rise, the carol, the creation," as Pound never does, since in the Cantos "the visions shimmer, float, harden, melt, spin, reflect, disperse, shoot away in vistas and expand in atmospheric sweeps, and then contract their focus on a bird or a plant or a face."

Of the main objections I have found to the Cantos, the first is to its materialism. But, contrary to general belief, in actual aesthetic products materialist and skeptical writers have considerably surpassed religious ones. This is hardly true of ancient Greece, where the greatest poets, Homer, Sappho, Aeschylus, Sophocles and Pindar, preceded the age of unbelief. One must remember, however, that it was far easier to be an aesthetic pagan than it is to be an aesthetic Christian. Apollo, Hermes and Aphrodite were really aesthetic beings, but one must have a marvelous eye for beauty to discover it in the Three Persons of the Godhead. Every Latin poet without exception was a materialist or skeptic. Catullus spoke for all when he said:

> Soles occidere et redire possunt;
> Nobis cum semel occidit brevis lux
> Nox est perpetua una dormienda.

In Italy, Dante was religious; but Petrarch, Politian, Ariosto, Machiavelli, Aretino and all the Renaissance poets were skeptical. Tasso lived under the Counterreformation, and was one of the first pupils of the Jesuits; so he may be called religious. That applies to Spain too. Cervantes, Calderon and Lope da Vega were not merely orthodox, but greatly approved the burning of heretics! In Germany, Schiller may have had a touch of religion, but Goethe was on the whole skeptical, and Lessing and Heine were the boldest of mockers. In France, nearly all the writers since Voltaire, whether in prose or verse, have been skeptics. I give my possible opponent Verlaine, however, unless he objects to taking him. In England, during the last couple of centuries, Shelley, Fitzgerald and Swinburne were skeptical enough, and where are there three religious poets to match them in aesthetic power? Tennyson alone can be named. It is a good deal to admit that the author of "In Memoriam" was a believer, but I can afford to be generous.

In truth, it is ridiculous to call even the nominally believing poets religious men. "The Blessed Damozel" is a poem about Heaven, but it is the very antithesis of a religious poem. The fact is that there has been unbroken enmity between religion and art. The Greeks in their best days were an exception, but even in Greece Plato at least appeared with his purer religion, and desired to expel poets and musicians from his republic. In Rome the fight of religion against the theater lasted almost till the end of the republic. To this day there are no bells in Muhammadan churches because Muhammad thought music wicked. In Italy beauty was worshipped by the bad Popes, but abhorred by the good ones. In the fifteenth century the Good Pope Paul II tortured and imprisoned poets, and next century the good Popes of the Counterreformation waged implacable war against poetry and art. In England the theaters were closed for many years, fiddlers were put in the stocks and poets had a narrow escape. In France Moliére could hardly get buried, and Lully was refused absolution till he burned an opera he had just composed. Even in the eighteenth century, the actress Le Couvreur was refused Christian burial, and had to be buried in a field for cattle. There is practically no form of art—neither music nor poetry nor dancing nor the drama nor the novel—which has not been persecuted for ages by every religion.

The second objection to the Cantos I have encountered is to the usury theme. It is suggested that this is a quite inadequate springboard for great poetry, and the importance he attaches to it shows a very serious flaw in Pound's scale of values. But those of us who, like Pound, have long been interested in the Money Question are familiar with the psychological barrier most people have in this respect. They are unable to contemplate the fact that we are potbound in an arbitrary and artificial money system which has no correspondence to reality at all. After all, as

Pound has said, an earlier Scotsman had anticipated the realization that lies at the root of Major C. H. Douglas' system. It is expressed in the phrase I italicize in the passage in which Pound says: "The Bank of England, a felonious combination, or, more precisely, a gang of usurers taking sixty per cent interest, was founded in 1694. Paterson, the founder of the Bank, clearly stated the advantages of his scheme: the bank hath the benefit of the interest on all moneys *which it creates out of nothing.*" It was on this basis that Major Douglas erected his charge that the issue and withdrawal of credit by the banking system does not reflect the physical realities of production and consumption, and that the theory of money so applied effects a continual and increasing indebtedness of the community to the banks. One debt cannot be liquidated without incurring a greater one. That is the lever of the Monopoly of Credit. The "Douglas Theorem" is that, owing to credit being treated as the property of the banks, a loan repayable on demand, instead of being administered as the money of the community held as a right, purchasing power is withdrawn from the public at a faster rate than it ceases to figure in the prices which the public has to meet if all its production is to be sold. That is to say, there enters into the costs of final products a fictitious element due entirely to the property conception of credit, an element which is fictitious in the sense that it does not represent the money equivalent of wealth consumed in making that product. In fact, the amount of credit withheld from the community in this way is approximately the money value of the net difference between its total production (capital and ultimate goods) and its consumption (final products bought and depreciation of real capital). This, it is claimed, is the irreducible cause of the inability to distribute the whole volume of consumable production which increases as the proportion of power equipment to labor increases. Hence the defeat by Money Monopoly of any benefit which would accrue to humanity by the replacement of human energy by natural power in production. As the products of one set of processes cannot be sold by the purchasing power distributed in respect of those processes, industrialism has only survived at all because the unsalable product of one period could be partly carried off by the credit distributed for inaugurating further production. So we are confronted with the logical but insane financial advice that the cure for an unsalable surplus is more production or economy. This is the very crux of the Money Monopoly. However successful man is in supplying his wants and saving his limbs, he must enjoy no relaxation of economic activity. In Major Douglas' words, as a mechanism for making work the financial system is as near perfect as possible, but as a means of distributing the products of what is now predominantly a natural-power productive plant, it fails completely. In fact, that is not its objective.

Major Douglas was not, however, prepared to accept this "philosophy" of economic activity as the chief end of man, and consequently—desiring *the economic independence and complete freedom of the individual*—made proposals for the return of credit to the people and the issue of national dividends as each citizen's share in the benefit of natural-power production. Major Douglas' proposals were in fact designed to answer the question which, with all their talk of freedom this and liberation that, the BBC and all the press and politicians ignore, namely: *And the liberty of not getting into debt—how about that?* A nation that will not get itself into debt drives the usurers to fury.

Listen to what Douglas himself said in a passage that strikes the very keynote of his philosophy (and incidentally aligns him with all that is best in Scottish thought from the Declaration of Arbroath to the present day):

> There probably never was a time in which disinterested legislation was so rare, just as there probably never was a device which was so effective in silencing criticism of interested legislation as this idea that self-interest on a worldly plane must necessarily be wicked. I would therefore make the suggestion in order to add to the gaiety of nations by creating a riot at once, that the first requisite of a satisfactory governmental system is that it shall divest itself of the idea that it has a mission to improve the morals or direct

the philosophy of any of its constituent citizens. Sir Walter Fletcher said: "We can find safety and progress only in proportion as we bring our methods of statecraft under the guidance of biological Truth." I think that this is one of those remarks which illuminate a subject much as the sky-line is illuminated on a dark night by a flash of summer lightning. *We know little about ourselves, and less about our neighbours, and almost nothing at all about the nature of a healthy Society. Nor do we display any particular anxiety to increase our knowledge in these directions.* Yet there is nowadays none so poor that he is not prepared to produce at short notice the plans which will put every human being in his place within the space of a few short weeks. . . . The physical scientist who wishes to obtain a sure foundation for the formulation of laws begins by standardising his re-agents. Temperature would be meaningless if we had not something we call "zero". But in regard to biology we are in a difficulty. We do not even know how unhealthy we are, though we have a strong suspicion that we are very sick indeed. To those, then, who are anxious to make a definite contribution to the saving of a sick world, it may not be impertinent to suggest that the natural creative forces of the universe might plausibly be expected to produce at least as good results if left alone to work themselves out through the agency of the individual, as may be expected from planning which is undertaken without any conception of the relation of the plan to the constitution and temperament of those who are affected. If all history and all observation has not been misread, there is implanted in the individual *a primary desire for freedom and security, which rightly considered are forms of the same thing*. There is no such thing as a freedom which is held upon terms, whether these terms are dictated by the State, by a banking system, or by a World Government. Until it can be shown that, with the resources which science has placed at his disposal, the individual is incapable of making freedom and security for himself, this multiplication of organisations whose interference we cannot avoid will only make a world catastrophe the more certain.

The values to be safeguarded in the Douglas Commonwealth are Liberty, Leisure and Culture. The will-to-plenty of the individual is to be given satisfaction, and the whole business and industrial life of society relegated to a subordinate place, somehow as in the economy of the human body many biological processes proceed automatically or semi-automatically, leaving the psychology of the human being free to develop its interests.

Systems were made for men, not men for systems (declared Major Douglas in the first chapter of his first book), and the interest of man, which is self-development, takes precedence over all systems, economic, political or theological. A ringing statement to come from an economist!

No wonder the newspapers gave him less obituary space than they accord to any footballer, film star or crooner. Douglas himself would not have been surprised at all. His entire propaganda was founded on the centuries-old recognition of the fact that *nescis, mi fili, quantilla prudentia mundus regatur* (You know, my son, with what a small stock of wisdom the world is governed). And he might have explained at any time during the twenty-odd years of our friendship, as another friend of mine did, viz., "God knows what gets into all governments at certain stages of their existence. It's easy to understand why Arab princes surround themselves with incompetents, eunuchs, dolts and degenerates, for Arab princes consider themselves infallible: whatever they do must of necessity be right. Consequently they elevate childhood friends or toadying relatives to the most important posts in their kingdoms. But only God knows why such things happen perpetually in countries regarded as politically enlightened, like England, France, America, supposedly governed by patriotic men. Yet they always have happened, and with horrifying frequency; the pages of history are sprinkled with dolts, idiots, drunkards maintained in the highest offices—mediocrities whose stubbornness has sacrificed armies, whose blindness has destroyed navies, whose bad judgment has ruined their countries' prestige, starved helpless people by the million, wrecked cities, toppled arts, civilization, learning and understanding in the dust—and most of these fools' names hold unsullied places in the lying annals of their respective nations."

If Douglas would not have been surprised at the scanty obituaries accorded him, there need be no surprise that Pound has not been given anything like his due and that the Cantos are condemned as incomprehensible patchworks. The reason is the same in both cases. So it is inevitable that a recent critic should be compelled to say:

> Over forty years ago, two Americans and an Irishman attempted to put English poetry back into the mainstream of European culture. The effect of these generations who have succeeded to the heritage of Eliot, Pound and Yeats has been largely to squander the awareness these three gave us of our place in world literature, and to retreat into a self-congratulatory parochialism. . . . Instead of the conscious formulation of a position, one has a provincial laziness of mind adopted as a public attitude and as the framework for an equally provincial verse. Against such a background poetic culture in Britain would seem to be living on an overdraft, the overdraft being the work of the writers of the older generation who are still with us.

It is true, as Emrys Humphreys said in a broadcast:

> It is not too soon to say that Joyce saved us from being smothered in the spurious; without Joyce, Eliot and Pound, the atmosphere of English literature today would be that of the bar of a suburban golf club. Honest, serious, sensitive communication would have become practically impossible. . . . The conditions of our time are fiercely inimical to the practice of the arts. Art: the very word invokes derision, contempt, suspicion, impatience.

Or as another recent writer (this time an American) puts it:

> The great surge of "modern" poetry in the English language in the second and third decades of this century was, except for Yeats, and Eliot since his transference of citizenship to England, largely American in its most forceful and influential aspects. Housman, Kipling, AE, Monro, Sassoon, Stephens, Aldington, de la Mare, Graves, the Sitwells—these names have loomed large at one time and have their places; a few have a distinguished place indeed. But the main drift has passed these writers by.

Precisely. Pound *is* the main drift.

A BUNDLE OF LETTERS

FROM RABINDRANATH TAGORE

> 508 W. High Street,
> Urbana, Illinois
> 5 Jan. 1913

Dear Mr. Ezra Pound

I send you the recent translations that I made here. I am not at all strong in my English grammar—please do not hesitate to make corrections when necessary. Then again I do not know the exact value of your English words. Some of them may have their souls worn out by constant use and some others may not have acquired their souls yet. So in my use of words there must be lack of proportion and appropriateness perhaps, that also could be amended by friendly hands.

> Yours very Sincerely
> Rabindranath Tagore

FROM T. S. ELIOT

> Merton College
> Oxford
> February 2 [1915]

My dear Pound

I am very glad to hear from you, and it is certainly very kind of you to make these efforts on my behalf. I enclose a copy of the Lady,[1] which seems cruder & awkwarder & more juvenile every time I copy it. The only enhancement which time has brought is the fact that by this time there are two or three other ladies who, if it is ever printed, may vie for the honour of having sat for it. It will please you, I hope, to hear that I had a Christmas card from the lady, bearing the "ringing greetings of friend to friend at this season of high festival." It seemed like old times.

[1] "Portrait of a Lady."

I must thank you again for your introduction to the Dolmetsch family—I passed one of the most delightful afternoons I have ever spent, in one of the most delightful households I have ever visited. You were quite right—there was no difficulty about the conversation, and I made friends with the extraordinary children in no time, and am wild to see them again. As for the dancing, they all danced (except the head of the family) for about an hour, I think, while I sat rapt. I have corresponded with Lewis, but his Puritanical Principles seem to bar my way to Publicity. I fear that King Bolo and his Big Black Kween will never burst into print. I understand that Priapism, Narcissism etc are not approved of, and even so innocent a rhyme as

>... pulled her stockings off
>   With a frightful cry of "Hauptbahnhof!!"

is considered decadent.

I have been reading some of your work lately. I enjoyed the article on the Vortex (please tell me who Kandinsky is). I distrust & detest Aesthetics, when it cuts loose from the Object, and vapours into the void, but you have not done that. The closer one keeps to the Artist's discussion of his technique the better, I think, and the only kind of art worth talking about is the art one happens to like. There can be no contemplative or easychair aesthetics, I think; only the aesthetics of the person who is about to do something. I was fearful lest you should hitch it up to Bergson or James or some philosopher, and was relieved to find that Vorticism was not a philosophy.

I hope that your work is progressing satisfactorily. I probably shall not be in town again until March. I hope that Yeats will still be there. Please remember me to Mrs. Pound.

Sincerely yours Thomas S. Eliot

James Joyce in Venice to Ezra Pound in London, 1915.

c/o Giovacchino Veneziani,
  Murano,
    Venice,
      (Italy,)

My dear Mr Pound

I am very glad to get your letter of ? inst and hope that you have now quite recovered from your illness. I have written to Mr Pinker and said that you will interview him. It is very kind of you to offer to do this for me and I shall be guided by you in the matter. The rest of the *Portrait of the Artist* had better be sent on to Grant Richards as soon as it is ready.

As regards rights Mr Grant Richards has [illegible] .... much better article, a letter, if he wishes not to conclude the open agreement about it. I am quite willing to entrust the disposal of the rights to Mr Pinker. Mr Grant Richards promised last July that he would give a definite answer within three weeks after the completed MS was in his possession. At least it seems to me that he did so but I cannot now find his letter.

My comedy *Exiles* is now finished but I should prefer to hold it up until my novel has been published in book form though I am willing to dispose of it also in the best way.

I believe, however, that the letter you send may have a good effect on Grant Richards. If you see Mr Pinker (I mean, of course, as soon as your illness allows you to go out of doors) you will perhaps explain to him why I have delayed in

112

answering his letter and why I am obliged to write in such a roundabout fashion.

I must say in conclusion that you are a very good correspondent for you always send me lively and good news. I hope you are living well in these bad times. I am still quite unmolested and hope to remain so but the situation is not very pleasant. I am glad also to hear that the *Egoist* still continues to appear and beg you to convey my kind regards to the editor whose letter I received and answered some time ago.

Very sincerely yours
James Joyce

17 March 1915

FROM WYNDHAM LEWIS

18 Fitzroy St.
Fitzroy Square.
W.C.

Friday. Dec. 31st [1915]

Dear Pound.

I have seen Miss Weaver. She appears to think that the book is too long to serialize, although she says they want a serial.[1] As to the possibility of bringing it out in volume form at once, that is reserved for Joyce's book;[2] so presumably Laurie has been guilty of a double mistake.

I have also read the first chapter of my book to Goldring. But I am afraid he is no good: he does not seem even able to get tick with his printer.

I saw Miss Weaver at 11 yesterday morning at Oakley House. I read her the first 4 pages, and then left off, as I was sure she would not like it, and we were in an empty room under depressing conditions. I did not leave the MS. with her: I thought I must make some further move with it. I cannot unfortunately afford to 'fold up my standards now, to unfurl them again on some brighter day' in King Ferdinand's words. I am afraid I may have bungled the Weaver business.

Many thanks for the cheque £15. You have taken out of Quinn's cheque the £8 for the Blasts? Did he say nothing of interest in his letter? If your Review is coming into being, you might, as you have said once or twice, find a little corner where my big book could creep.

I may see you on your return from your holiday.

Yrs
Wyndham Lewis

---

[1] This refers to Lewis' novel *Tarr*, which Miss Weaver finally accepted in January, 1916, for serial publication in the *Egoist*.

[2] *Portrait of the Artist*.

A Bundle of Letters
FROM JAMES JOYCE

                                      Pension Villa Rossa
                                      Locarno
                                      Switzerland
                                      [1917]

Dear Pound: I came here a few days ago but was so busy looking after luggage etc that I could not write. It is useless to go into the subject of my physical and financial collapse in August. As regards the former what is done is done. I cannot see very well even yet but the sight gets better. About the latter I owe you and Miss Weaver very much for your prompt kindness. But for you I should have been derelict. I notice that you blame yourself for having misled me. The stupidity, however, is at my end. I am glad *Ulysses* is to appear in both reviews from March on and now that I can read and write again I shall get to work. I hope you will both like it. I send you a copy of *Marzocco* with an article by Mr Diego Angeli. The Manager of Messrs Crès and Co spoke to me about a French translation of my novel (to be published in the course of the present century) and Dostoyevsky's daughter was here yesterday. She has read Mr Angeli's article and wants a copy of the book. She will have to print one for herself, I fear. My wife told me you are bringing out a book with an essay in it about the novel. It may interest therefore to hear that after the first edition had been sold out and the book reviewed in eight countries the printers wrote asking the writer to delete and alter passages in it and refused to print even the second edition. I believe Miss Weaver has found some printer in the country who will do it, he says. I am now correcting proofs of *Exiles*. Yeats wrote to me about it but he seems to have forgotten what it is about. In any case he says his theatre is passing through a crisis. The actors he has now cannot even play low comedy. In the hope that things may have improved I am writing to him again about it rather pressingly. I am also going to write to Mr Martyn though I do not know him. If their theatre has no actors to play it surely they could be trained. If not what are they doing on the stage? I shall write also to Mr Sturge Moore who, you said, liked it and to Mr Archer again and to Mr [name illegible] and possibly to Mr Short, Mr Barker and Mr Symons. In fact, as usual, I shall write a great number of letters to a great number of people.

I got copies of *Little Review* with your amusing and high-spirited lines. The review looks more prosperous since you took over the European editorship.

I hope Mrs Pound and yourself are quite well. This letter, tardy as it is, is not very long or even complete but sometimes I find it difficult to keep my eyes open—like the readers of my masterpieces.

I have the impression that I am forgetting to tell you many things. No doubt I shall remember them five minutes after having posted this letter. I got Mr Eliot's verses only this morning.

Accept my very sincere thanks however lamely expressed, for having helped me at such a difficult moment.

Yours very gratefully
James Joyce

FROM MARIANNE MOORE

14 St. Luke's Place,
New York City,
January 9, 1919.

Dear Mr. Pound:

In your letter of December 16th,[1] I have a great deal to thank you for. My contemporaries are welcome to anything they have come upon first and I do not resent unfriendly criticism, much less that which is friendly.

---

[1] *Letters of Ezra Pound*, ed. by D. D. Paige (New York: Harcourt, Brace & Company, 1950). Letter No. 155.

I am glad to give you personal data and hope that the bare facts that I have to offer, may not cause work that I may do from time to time, utterly to fail in interest. Even if they should, it is but fair that those who speak out, should not lie in ambush. I was born in 1887 and brought up in the home of my grandfather, a clergyman of the Presbyterian church. I am Irish by descent, possibly Scotch also, but purely Celtic, was graduated from Bryn Mawr in 1909 and taught shorthand, typewriting and commercial law at the government Indian School in Carlisle, Pennsylvania, from 1911 until 1915. In 1916, my mother and I left our home in Carlisle to be with my brother—also a clergyman—in Chatham, New Jersey—but since the war, Chaplain of the battleship Rhode Island and by reason of my brother's entering the navy, my mother and I are living at present in New York, in a small apartment. Black Earth, the poem to which I think you refer, was written about an elephant that I have, named Melancthon; and contrary to your impression, I am altogether a blond and have red hair.

The first writing I did was a short story published in 1907 by the Bryn Mawr undergraduate monthly and during 1908 and nine, I assisted with the editing of the magazine and contributed verse to it.

Any verse that I have written, has been an arrangement of stanzas, each stanza being an exact duplicate of every other stanza. I have occasionally been at pains to make an arrangement of lines and rhymes that I liked, repeat itself, but the form of the original stanza of anything I have written has been a matter of expediency, hit upon as being approximately suitable to the subject. The resemblance of my progress to your beginnings is an accident so far as I can see. I have taken great pleasure in both your prose and your verse, but it is what my mother terms the saucy parts, which have most fixed my attention. In 1911, my mother and I were some months in England and happening into Elkin Mathews's shop, were shown photographs of you which we were much pleased to see. I like a fight but I admit that I have at times objected to your promptness with the cudgels. I say this merely to be honest. I have no Greek, unless a love for it may be taken as a knowledge of it and I have not read very voraciously in French; I do not know Ghil and La Forgue and know of no tangible French influence on my work. Gordon Craig, Henry James, Blake, the minor prophets and Hardy, are so far as I know, the direct influences bearing on my work.

I do not appear. Originally, my work was refused by the Atlantic Monthly and other magazines and recently I have not offered it. My first work to appear outside of college was a poem, which one of three, I do not recall—published by the Egoist in 1915 and shortly afterward, four or five poems of mine were published by Poetry, a fact which pleased me at the time, but one's feeling changes and not long ago when Miss Monroe invited me to contribute, I was not willing to. Alfred Kreymborg has been hospitable and does not now shut the door to me and Miss Anderson has been most kind in sending me copies of a number of The Little Review in which some lines of mine have appeared with which I am wholly dissatisfied. Moreover, I am not heartily in sympathy with the Little Review though I have supported other magazines for which less could be said. I grow less and less desirous of being published, produce less and have a strong feeling for letting alone what little I do produce. My work jerks and rears and I cannot get up enthusiasm for embalming what I myself, accept conditionally.

Anything that is a stumbling block to my reader, is a matter of regret to me and punctuation ought to be exact. Under ordinary circumstances, it is as great a hardship to me to be obliged to alter punctuation as to alter words, though I will admit that at times I am heady and irresponsible.

I like New York, the little quiet part of it in which my mother and I live. I like to see the tops of the masts from our door and to go to the wharf and look at the craft on the river.

I do not feel that anything phenomenal is to be expected of New York and I sometimes feel as if there are too many captains in one boat, but on the whole, the amount of steady co-operation that is to be counted on in the interest of getting things launched, is an amazement to me. I am interested to know of your having had a hand in the publishing of T. S. Eliot. I like his work. Over here, it strikes me that there is more evidence of power among painters and sculptors than among writers.

I am glad to have you send the prose to the Egoist and to have you keep the two poems that you have, for your quarterly. As soon as I have it, I shall send you something new. Perhaps you would be interested in seeing a poem which I have just given to one of our new magazines here, a proposed experiment under the directon of Maxwell Bodenheim, and a poem of mine which appeared in the Bryn Mawr college Lantern last year?

To capitalize the first word of every line, is rather slavish and I have substituted small letters for capitals in the enclosed versions of the two poems you have.

I fully agree with you in what you say about the need of being more than defensible when giving offense. I have made

> You are right, that swiftmoving sternly
> Intentioned swaybacked baboon is nothing to you and the chimpanzee?

to read

> You are right about it; that wary,
> Presumptuous young baboon is nothing to you and the chimpanzee?

For

> And the description is finished. Of the jaguar with the pneumatic Feet,

read

> What is there to look at? And of the leopard, spotted underneath and on its toes:

Leopards are not spotted underneath, but in old illuminations they are, and on Indian printed muslins, and I like the idea that they are.

its-self may read its self

and I have made

> The little dish, dirt brown, mulberry
> White, powder blue or oceanic green—is half human and any
> > Thing peacock is "divine."

to read

> the little dishes, brown, mulberry
> or sea green are half human and waiving the matter of artistry,
> > anything which can not be reproduced, is "divine."

Confusion is created by introducing contradictory references to lizards; I have therefore left out stanzas seven and eight and I have made other alterations.

In *A Graveyard,* I have made *is* to end the line as you suggest and for the sake of symmetry, have altered the arrangement of lines in the preceding stanzas. I realize that by writing consciousness and volition, emphasis is obtained which is sacrificed by retaining the order which I have, and I am willing to make the change, though I prefer the original order.

Sincerely yours,
Marianne Moore

FROM HENRY NEWBOLT

Netherhampton House,
Salisbury.
[1920?]

My dear Pound,

Thank you—if I were to measure your pleasure by my own I should give you credit for a good deal. But I don't plead guilty to the charge of blindness or deafness: I have all your books (some by your own gift) except the American one & I know this many years some of your poems by heart. The choice at which you chafe—or wonder—was not without a reason at the back of it. I *like* these poems—isn't that almost enough?—but the actual reason was that they were liked—the sonnets in particular—by Robert Bridges who praised them to me years ago.

Well, I am most anxious to do what the poet wisely prefers. I don't want, if I can help it, to include poems pub' —only in the U.S.A. But if you will allow me I will make this proposal. Will you send me your consent as speedily as possible to my using 5 poems taken out of your English publications (Umbra and the older ones) and I will agree to pay you £10. 10. 0 for them. Further, if you have a copy you can send me of a suitable later poem, I will do my best to get it in either in place of one of the 5 or in addition to them, & in the latter case at the same rate.

You are, in your turn, out of date about us & our views over here. We care not a boterflie nor a bene whether a poem is in rhyme or not. Our young poets are much less learned than you but far more adventurous. Their great idea is to be quit of "technique", & they wd. shudder at your talk of "15 years work".

Yours very sincerely,
Henry Newbolt.

FROM W. B. YEATS

October 7 [1920]

4, Broad Street,
Oxford

Dear Ezra

Here is an essay, which I hope you will send to "The Dial" for me. When I was in USA they said they would be glad of it, so I have corrected it & re-written the end at some length. I think under the circumstances, though it appeared in Ireland in "The Irish Statesman" they might pay me something for it.

I go to Dublin at the week end for a couple of weeks to have my throat operated upon.

I have just finished a long poem, 100 lines, & I think it good, at least as good as "The Prayer for my Daughter" & much the same sort of thing. It describes Horton & Mrs. Emery & MacGregor.[1]

Yours
W. B. Yeats

FROM RICHARD ALDINGTON

Malthouse Cottage
Padworth
Nr Reading
Berks.
England.
7/8/28

Dear Ezra,

Very glad indeed to have your card and to know that you don't wholly disapprove of the Gourmont book.[2] I hear that in New York some of the "critics" think I have cut too much. Personally I don't think so, but I'd very much like to know whether you think I have omitted much of importance. Naturally, everyone has his own opinion as to what ought to go in, but I read Remy through twice before starting the book, and managed to get in everything I wanted.

Did you see the article on modern American Literature in the Mercure of 15th July? They talked about modern American poetry and Imagism without mentioning your name! Gave all the credit to Amy. This was too much, so Franky[3] and I each concocted a letter and fired it off to Valette. They ought to appear in the 15th August edition.

---

[1] "All Souls' Night," Epilogue to "A Vision," *The Tower.*

[2] *Remy de Gourmont,* selected and trans. by Aldington. Pound reviewed it for the *Dial* (January, 1929) under the heading "Mr. Aldington's Views on Gourmont."

[3] F. S. Flint.

Would you like me to send a protest to Transition as well? I imagine Michaud (the article writer) is a friend of Jolas, since he appears in the last Transition and puffs Jolas's anthology in the N.R.F. I wrote and told Jolas that in his book he is wrong to date your influence from 1916; it should be 1912.

Glenn Hughes is coming to Europe on a Guggenheim scholarship to "write a book on Imagism and allied poetic movements in Europe, with the collaboration of the principal poets concerned."[1] He is coming to stay with me directly he gets to England, and I will keep a fairly tight hand on him here, to prevent "contamination". Probably the best thing will be for us all to see him and give him our own dope. Hughes's book will be published by Gugg funds probably, and should do some good. Is there no way by which you, H.D. and I can agree on an official version of the origins of Imagism, to which Frank and Fletcher would subscribe? H.D. won't know me because (so I'm told) she thinks I want to harm her—Christ knows why, since I feel perfectly benevolent and wouldn't hurt her for anything. Are you allowed to know her? Anyway, the principal thing is for you and I to agree and put the dope on Hughes. My version is that Hulme was a sort of distant ancestor, that you invented Imagism as a word, that the "movement" was decided upon by the three of us, at your suggestion, in a Kensington tea-shop, to launch H.D. We all published "Imagist" poems with Harriet before Amy was heard of. The first Imagist anthology was your idea and edited by you. Amy only came in as an after-thought, and you will perhaps remember that we argued about it in a taxi on the way to the Berkeley. Then, you wanted to push on to new things, and Amy regrouped the survivors, and nominally edited the other three anthologies; though, in fact, each poet chose his own work. Amy undoubtedly put Imagism over to the public, but if we'd owned New England cotton mills and only spoken to God, no doubt we could have done likewise.

Shall I send Hughes down to see you sometime this win-

---

[1] *Imagism and the Imagists* (Stanford: Stanford University Press, 1931).

ter? I may be in the Sth of France myself, and would pilot him along possibly. Have you got the original Imagist "Documents"—I mean early issues of "Poetry", early Little Reviews, and the like? Also Frankie's article and your "don'ts"?[1] I think Hughes ought to reproduce all these— including the first poems we each had in Poetry. For the allied movement, I suggest Tom, Read and the Sitwells in England. "Wheels" was evidently a crib of the Imagist anthologies, and the dates on title-pages do not lie. Then he can paddle in with les jeunes in Paris. (He's got to have somebody else in the book, and if he can attach 'em all to our tails, tant mieux.)

I saw some of les jeunes in Paris—amusing but a bit thin, I thought. Missed Hemingway and Antheil. Saw Joyce. By the way, didn't I return to you those letters of his to the Brit Consul in Geneva? If not, I've lost 'em. I think Joyce is slightly peeved about it. Have a look through your papers, and see if you got 'em.

The N.R.F. are going Surrealiste, with a special cult for Aragon.

           Au revoir, ever yours,

                      R

FROM WILLIAM CARLOS WILLIAMS

        William Carlos Williams, M.D.
             9 Ridge Road
            Rutherford, N.J.

                          Nov. 6, 1928

Dear Ezrie:

Nothing will ever be said of better understanding regarding my work than your article in The Dial.[2] I must thank you for your great interest and discriminating defense of my position. Without question you have hit most of the trends that I am following with the effect that you have

---

[1] "A Few Don'ts by an Imagiste," *Poetry*, March, 1913.

[2] "Dr. Williams' Position," *Dial*, November, 1928.

clarified my designs on the future which in turn will act as encouragement and strength for me.

Naturally I consider myself a fool for not getting out of Medicine. I do not consider myself a fool for having been a physician for the past twenty years. That was accurately figured out in its relations to my disposition and mental capabilities. It has all turned out precisely as I foresaw, save only that at my present age I planned to withdraw from active competition wth the world and close up the gaps in my expositions, continuing at this till I was shovelled under or went daffy or satisfactorily convinced myself that I had failed.

I am now engaged in cutting out much of my medical work under the guise of becoming a "specialist". Within a few months I will have done with evening office hours, that hellish drag. But it is not going fast enough. I can't quit cold for I would only torment myself into the grave if I did so. I ain't built that way, I mean to withstand financial worries or to discover ways of living aside from the work of my hands. I simply can't.

But things are moving nevertheless according to the plans. Perhaps I expect too much.

But I am touched by the sobriety of your review, that is what I set out to say meaning to add that I am going on as best I can and that you have helped me there also. You also have grown older—without loss. In fact I like your writing in what you have said of me as well as anything I have seen of yours in prose.

I have the new Cantos but there has been no time in which to read—as yet.

     Yours

       Bill

FROM FORD MADOX FORD

> FORD MADOX FORD
> VILLA PAUL, CHEMIN
> DE LA CALADE, CAP
> BRUN, TOULON, VAR
>
> 6th June 1931

Dear Ezra,

This is to authorise and empower you without let, hindrance, fee, honorarium, deodand, infangtheff, utfangtheff freely to translate or cause to be betrayed any work of mine save only my commentary on the Book of Genesis into any tongue or language save only the dialects of the Isle of Man and of the City of Philadelphia, Pa in its pre-1909 variety or sameness.

We may shortly be passing through Genoa and would like you to lunch with us at any there hostelry designated by you.

I had yesterday the agreeable news that my latest novel is a best seller in New York. As however the largest sale of any book in that city has not yet exceeded four hundred copies this year and since no publisher has more than $11 in his bank I do not—though they need it—propose to have the seats of my pants reinforced.

May God and your country pass you by in their judgments is the prayer of

> FMF

FROM E. E. CUMMINGS

[1935]

Dear Thunderer

many thanks for the Ezra Shrapnel! it arrived, avec excellent rabbitman's Honest Obus, from Nott (positively).[1]

---

[1] This refers apparently to Pound's two pamphlets: *Alfred Venison's Poems* and *Social Credit: An Impact*, published by Stanley Nott, London, 1935.

Of what I can understand—as you would say—enjoyed peculiarly "god or no god" passage: and a sketch about her sloppin' soul.

Met Joe[1] il y a quesques jours &, b jeezuz, never have I beheld a corpse walking . . . said he was planning to go "on relief" as there seemed nothing else for it. Told me he'd been previously deterred by fact that already "on relief" are 2 classes—"the kind of people you wouldn't be found dead with and the kind of people who need it so much more than we do" (sic). Alleged his failure to comply with an ancient suggestion of mine and write yourself was due to lack of a 5 cent postagestamp; but I wouldn't let the devil himself get away with that, so am a nickel worthier. I mentioned Messer G "Esquire" to Joe and he brightened. Then, taking the horns by the bull, I flew a 2nd article toward Chicago: & this despite fact that my twain letters to aforesaid ridactur stay unanswered, or in other words, nobody asked me to do nawthing els. As postscript to missive accompanying the dit article I furnished Master Gould's whereabouts, towit: Central Hotel, 149 East 14th Street

Elizabeth, my sister, works for the "COS" (Charity Organization Society). Her business is to struggle with bums & plutocrats. She makes the latter turn on people's gas when bills aren't properly paid at 10 below zero etc . . . The former sometimes try to convert her to communism, sometimes threaten her with razors. But what I thought you'd like to hear is something else: the other day, for the first time in her career, she was stopped cold—hitherto, whenever somebody called up and wanted a handsome man to mind an airdale or a mechanic familiar with the vertebrae of Zeppelins or a professor to teach Esquimaux or a deserving pregnancy or whathaveyou, she's just dipped into the unemployed and fished up a little bit of all right; but now comes a voice demanding, on behalf of a huge radio-network-act "a whole family with coughs, NOT CONTAGIOUS; to cough into the microphone" . . .

[1] Joe Gould

"   words better left unsaid
Come back to grieve us when we think them dead"
(James Boyle O'Reilly) on which I was brought up; but also on Plato's Republic fortunately comma My sister Elizabeth says that if Joe can only keep on relief for a few years he'll have a new set of somebody's teeth; I can't believe it. As a single man, she says, he ought to get $5 every two weeks for food (& something a month for rent): that I can believe.

Apparently poverty is not doing what you want to whereas riches are doing what you don't
  yrs for whatever's at rightangles to both.

eec

EZRA POUND AND THE FRENCH LANGUAGE

by William Fleming

Obviously, a writer such as Ezra Pound—who, as T. S. Eliot has pointed out, is more responsible for the revolution in twentieth-century poetry than any other individual—can hardly be "accounted for" in terms of any of the particular "influences" at one time or another affecting him. His reading has been wide, acute his sense of what really matters in that reading. Behind that, as well, has stood his own remarkable originality: from an early age he appears to have clearly known what he wanted, and simply then to have set out and found it.

Nevertheless, there is profit for the less endowed—particular profit in this case—in examining Pound's dialogue with French literature—a lifelong dialogue, as I shall proceed to show—not only for its own intrinsic interest but also that we may discern what elements of that literature he contrived to bring over into English that were not there before—or at least not at the time of his commencing his career—and, more importantly, the extent to which these elements have been made strictly compatible with the English tradition. The profit is particular because French culture has ultimately come to mean more to Pound than the culture associated with any other language;

in which generalization I am forced to include even English—as I shall proceed to show.

Two aspects have to be considered: the direct influence of particular French writers and, less obvious but utterly central, the indirect affect of the culture, the language itself.

In the first respect, which is important enough, goodness knows, we are fortunate in having available to us Pound's own considered view of what he has owed—or rather *not* owed—to particular French poets of the late nineteenth century, the period naturally of immediate relevance. I quote at length from his 1928 letter, written in French, to René Taupin:[1]

> ... En 1908-9 à Londres (avant le début de H. D.): cènacle T. E. Hulme, Flint, D. Fitzgerald, moi, etc. Flint, beaucoup français-fé, jamais arrivé à condensation. $\left\{\begin{array}{l}\text{concentration}\\\text{avoir centre}\end{array}\right\}$ Symbolistes francais>'90's à Londres....
> Influence fr. sur moi—relativement tard.
> Rapports fr.>eng. via Arthur Symons etc. 1890. Baudelaire, Verlaine, etc.
> ... Certes, progrès du *technique* poétique.—Fr. en avant. Gautier 'Albertus', England 1890-1908. Ce que Rimbaud atteint par intuition (génie) dans certains poèms, érigé en esthétique conscient (?? peut-être) —je ne veux pas prendre une gloire injuste—mais pour tant que je sais. J'en ai fait une esthétique plus ou moins systématique—et j'ai pu citer certains poèmes de R. comme exemple. (*Mais* aussie certains poèms de Catulle.)
> Et c'est certain que à part certains procédés d'expression —R. et moi n'avons point de rassemblance. Mais presque *toute* l'experiméntation, technique en poésie de 1830— jusqu'à moi—était faite en France.
> Avec toute modestie, je crois que j'étais orienté avant de connaître les poètes français modernes. Que j'ai profité de leurs inventions techniques (comme Edison ou aucun autre homme de science profite des découvertes). Y'a, aussi, les anciens: Villon, les Troubadours.

[1] From *The Letters of Ezra Pound*, ed. by D. D. Paige, copyright 1950 by Harcourt, Brace & World, Inc., and reprinted with their permission.

Vous trouverez en mon *The Spirit of Romance,* publié 1910, ce que je savais avant d'aborder les Fr. modernes.

... Pour y revenir: Je crois que la poésie français soit *très* difficilement racine d'une bon poésie anglaise ou américaine, *mais* que la *technique* des poètes français était *certainment* en état de servir d'*éducation* aux poètes de ma langue—du temps de Gautier jusqu'à 1912.

Que les poètes *essentiels,* à cette étude, se réduisent à Gautier, Corbière, Laforgue, Rimbaud. Que depuis Rimbaud, aucun poète en France n'a inventé rien de fondamental . . . .

Je crois que Eliot, dont les premières poésies ont montré influence de Laforgue, a moins de respect pour Laf. que le respect que j'ai pour Laf.

Gautier j'ai étudié et je le révère. Ce que vous prenez pour influence de Corbière est probablement influence directe de Villon . . . .

Ma *réforme:*
1. Browning—dénué des paroles superflues
2. Flaubert—mot juste, présentation ou constatation

Réforme métrique plus profonde—date de 1905 on commence avant de connaître Fr. moderne . . . .

As Pound has never been one to conceal his debts, the above statement can be accepted at its face value. The qualifications to observe are three: (1) that Pound is here restricting his consideration to poetry; (2) that he is considering particularly French poets post-Baudelaire; and (3) that though certain influences may have arrived "late," they may nevertheless have been important in contributing to his full maturity, which is, after all, what is important to us.

Let us review the chronology. Pound permanently left America and settled in London in late 1908; he was then twenty-two. It is not without relevance that this first decisive step in his literary career coincides exactly in time with what can be described as the "honeymoon" period in French/English political and social relationships. This was the era of Edward VII, of the so long withheld *rapprochement,* of the cementing of the Entente Cordiale. He came to a literary society made up largely, in fact, of Francophiles.

His own tastes at that stage, as evidenced by his first published poetry and by his 1910 *The Spirit of Romance,* were, however, already formed—in strength. He reserved his enthusiasm only for the perfect in the classic sense—for, specifically, Catullus, Martial, Dante, the Troubadours and Villon, finding in these poets a seriousness, a hardness and accuracy of expression that he opposed to the softness and amateurishness of late-Victorian English verse. In the later-written *The ABC of Reading* (1934) he restates, in most explicit language, the permanent validity for him of, above all, François Villon: "The hardest, the most authentic, the most absolute poet of France."

However, his overall attitude to French literature at this period, so far as he was then acquainted with it, was ambivalent. (He had first come in contact with *modern* French, it appears, in company with Mathurin Dondo during a visit to France in 1906.) On the one hand he had no use for the "smelling of talcum" aspect of much recent French verse, while on the other, omitting the special case of Villon, he gloried in the neatness and limpidity of early French. In this respect, he was still at that time at the mercy of only that version of modern French which the leading English writers immediately before him had been able to assimilate.

Let me illustrate. Here is a passage in which Oscar Wilde expresses *his* appreciation (without direct acknowledgment, by the way) of Huysman; it appears in his novel *The Picture of Dorian Gray,* published in 1891:

> His eye fell on the yellow book that Lord Henry had sent him.... After a few minutes he became absorbed.... The style in which it was written was that curious jewelled style, vivid and obscure at once, full of argot and of anachronisms, of technical expressions and of elaborate paraphrases.... There were in it metaphors as monstrous as orchids, and as subtle in colour. The life of the senses was described in the terms of mystical philosophy. One hardly knew at times whether one was reading the spiritual ecstasies of some mediaeval saint, or the morbid confessions of a modern sinner.... The mere cadence of the sentences,

the subtle monotony of their music . . . produced . . . a form of reverie, a malady of dreaming . . . .

Alongside of which we may also place *Hallucination:1,* written at about the same period by the "advanced" and influential Arthur Symons:

> One petal of a blood-red tulip pressed
> Between the pages of a Baudelaire:
> No more; and I was suddenly aware
> Of the white fragrant apple of a breast
> On which my lips were pastured . . . .
> . . . Then as my mouth grew parched, stung as with fire
> By that white fragrant apple, once so fair,
> That seemed to shrink and spire into a flame,
> I cried, and wakened, crying on your name:
> One blood-red petal stained the Baudelaire.

To see how Pound reacted, we have only to posit his remark in *The Spirit of Romance:* "In Villon filth is filth, crime is crime; neither crime nor filth is gilded. They are not considered as strange delights and forbidden luxuries, accessible only to wanton spirits. . . ." I believe it was largely because of such an immediate background that Pound has seemingly failed all his life to respond to the genius of, in particular, Baudelaire, Mallarmé and Verlaine, the French poets his predecessors especially admired.

At the same time, of course, he could not *altogether* escape the French flavor universally emanated by most of the best English writers of the period, such as Swinburne, Rosetti, Yeats, Ernest Dowson, Lionel Johnson and Arthur Symons—nor really, I suppose, would he have wanted to. Certain more general elements—irony, sophistication, the *poésie de villes,* a growing sense of professionalism—were owed, after all, to France and were quite readily taken up and incorporated by Pound. Here then he might have left it, picking up the little "modernism" he found useful and proceeding on his own way under his classical and medieval models.

Fortunately, however, he came at this time to fall under the direct personal influence of the prose writer and editor

Ford Madox Hueffer (later called Ford Madox Ford), who was then conducting in London a campaign to bring into English the workmanship, clarity and professionalism he believed were preeminently represented in the work of Flaubert and certain other nineteenth-century French novelists; that is, in French *prose* writers. So important was this campaign that even many years later—in 1937, to be precise—Pound insisted, "The revolution of the world began so far as it affected the men who were of my age in London in 1908, with the LONE whimper of Ford Madox Hueffer." It was Ford above all others who was instrumental in introducing Pound to what was really significant (given the context of the times) in French literature—its accuracy, its precision of rendering, its verbal drama; and this, note well, needed to be approached first—just as chronologically it came to occur—in its prose, not in its verse.

Pound's discovery of Flaubert has remained central to his thinking and his poetic practice since; one thinks, for instance, of the juxtapositions and orchestration of the Agricultural Show chapter of *Madame Bovary,* and its relevance to the method of the Cantos. Further, from that time on, it became nearly impossible for Pound to write even a page of criticism without referring to the centrality of Flaubert. And, equally beside, stands his associated regard for Stendhal, whose normalcy of style ("flatness") he came to contrast with the "originality" usually sought after by English stylists. In fact, in an essay written in 1913 (and he has repeated this view in later books) he dated the revitalization of writing in recent times from that moment in nineteenth-century France when prose became the more important art, a moment prefigured in Stendhal's passage which he quoted there in full (and not for the first time):

> La poésie, avec ses comparaisons obligées, sa mythologie que ne croit pas le poète, sa dignité de style à la Louis XIV, et tout l'attirail de ses ornements appelés poétiques, est bien audessous de la prose dès qu'il s'agit de donner une idée claire et précise des mouvements du coeur; or, dans ce genre, on n'émeut que par la clarté.

". . . une idée claire et précise . . ."—we shall have reason to come back to this concept later.

It was in the few years immediately following this eye-opener from Ford that Pound underwent his most intense phase of development. Thoroughly immersed then in the brilliant vortex that was prewar London, he founded the Imagiste school, met and collaborated with Wyndham Lewis and T. S. Eliot, got James Joyce launched, began his assimilation of Professor Fenollosa's work on Chinese poetry, collaborated with W. B. Yeats on the Japanese Noh drama translations and, concurrently, undertook on his own account a *really* close study of post-Baudelaire French poetry, at the same time setting in order all his ideas on these matters in a series of critical notes which, after the years, still pulse with excitement.

This same period, moreover—that is, from about 1910 to about 1920—saw for Pound, insofar as poetry is concerned, the publication of *Ripostes* (his first "modern" book: 1912), *Cathay* (his first Chinese translations: 1915), *Lustra* (the full flowering of his modern interests: 1916), *Homage to Sextus Propertius* (1917), the first three Cantos (1917) and the great *Hugh Selwyn Mauberley* (1920). Besides, he concurrently began, in a series of letters to Iris Barry opened in 1916, an orderly formulation of his critical views on the whole tradition and on the nature of poetry which were eventually to mature in the very important 1928 essay entitled "How to Read" (elaborated later in the 1934 book *The ABC of Reading*).

Let us make a closer examination of this central period of his career, with particular reference to its component of French. Before quoting from his own appreciations of French poets crystallized at that time—this is obviously better than second-hand characterizations—, it is desirable that we have at hand first an important dissociation he made later, its most concise expression being in his 1942 Italian pamphlet *Carta Da Visita* (translated by John Drummond):

For those without access to my criticism in English, I

repeat: the art of poetry is divisible into *phanopoeia, melopoeia,* and *logopoeia.* Verbal composition, that is to say, is formed of words which evoke or define visual phenomena, of words which register or suggest auditory phenomena (i.e., which register the various conventional sounds of the alphabet and produce, or suggest, a raising or lowering of the tone which can sometimes be registered more accurately by musical notation), and, thirdly, of a play or 'dance' among the concomitant meanings, customs, usages, or implied contexts of the words themselves.

Here, then, is his considered on-the-spot attitude to post-Baudelaire French poets, taken from his 1918 study; of what they must have meant to his own practice, his tone amply attests:

> ... We may take it that Gautier achieved hardness in *Emaux et Camées* ....
>
> After Gautier, France produced, as nearly as I can understand, three chief and admirable poets: Tristan Corbière, perhaps the most poignant writer since Villon; Rimbaud, a vivid and induitable genius; and Laforgue—a slighter, but in some ways a finer 'artist' than either of the others. ... Rimbaud's effects seem to come often as the beauty of certain silver crystals produced by chemical means. Laforgue always knows what he is at; Rimbaud, the 'genius', in the narrowest and deepest sense of the term, the 'most modern', seems, almost without knowing it, to hit on the various ways in which the best writers were to follow him, slowly. Laforgue is the 'last word': out of infinite knowledge of all the ways of saying a thing he finds the right way ....
>
> Corbière seems to me the greatest poet of the period ....
>
> Laforgue conveys his content by comment, Corbière by ejaculation, as if the words were wrenched and knocked out of him by fatality; by the violence of his feeling, Rimbaud presents a thick suave colour, firm, even.

It might be noted that of no English poet, save perhaps Chaucer, has he ever penned such praise. The more amplified statement in the later "How to Read" (1928)—after he was deeply launched into the Cantos—evidences no diminution of regard:

Author's corrected typescript of Homage to Sextus Propertius, *1917.*

She was veiled in the midst of that place,
Damp wooly handkerchiefs were stuffed into her undryable eyes,
And a querulous noise responded to our solicitous reprobations.

     For which things you will get a reward from me
          Lygdamus?
To say many things is equal to having a home.

And the other woman has not noticed me
    by her pretty manners,
"She has caught me with herbaceous poison,
   she twiddles the spiked wheel of a rhombus,
"She stews puffed frogs, snakes' bones, the moulded feathers of
        screech owls,
"She binds me with ravvles of shrouds.
  "Black spiders spin in her bed.
"Let her lovers snore at her in the morning!
  "May the gout cramp up her feet!
  "Does he like me to sleep here alone, Lygdamus?
  "Will he say nasty things at my funeral?".

And you expect me to believe this ...
   after twelve nights of discomfort?

The first separate edition of a Canto, distributed gratis, London, 1919.

THE FOURTH CANTO

by

EZRA POUND

Forty
Copies of this poem, numbered 1-40
on Japanese Vellum set up and privately printed
by John Rodker. Completed
Oct:4 1919
This is No. 9

THE OVID PRESS

A notebook jotting by Pound, used in "Canto VI."

Roladini
=
1200 – 1260
cont aufway.

mandato Ecelini
sui patris, Sordellus
de ipsius familia
Dnm ipsam latenter
a marito subtraxit
cum qua in patris
Curia permanente
dictum fuit ipsum
Sordellum concubuisse
et ~~ipso~~ ipso
expulso ab Ecelino

During the nineteenth century the superiority, if temporary, is at any rate obvious, and to such a degree that I believe no man can write really good verse unless he knows Stendhal and Flaubert. Or, let us say, *Le Rouge et le Noir,* the first half of *La Chartreuse, Madame Bovary, L'Education, Les Trois Contes, Bouvard et Pécuchet.* To put it perhaps more strongly, he will learn more about the art of charging words from Flaubert than he will from the floribund sixteenth century dramatists . . . .

In France, as the novel developed, spurred on, shall we say, by the activity in the prose-media, the versifyers were not idle.

Departing from *Albertus,* Gautier developed the medium we find in the *Emaux et Camées.* England in the 'nineties had got no further than the method of the *Albertus.* If Corbière invented no process he at any rate restored French verse to the vigour of Villon and to an intensity that no Frenchman had touched during the intervening four centuries.

Unless I am right in discovering *logopoeia* in Propertius (which means unless the academic teaching of Latin displays crass insensitivity as it probably does), we must say that Laforgue invented *logopoeia* . . . . And Rimbaud brought back to *phanopoeia* its clarity and directness.

All four of these poets, Gautier, Corbière, Laforgue, Rimbaud, redeem poetry from Stendhal's condemnation. There is in Corbière something one finds nowhere before him, unless in Villon.

Laforgue is not like any preceding poet . . . .

In Rimbaud the image stands clean, unencumbered by non-functioning words; to get anything like this directness of presentation one must go back to Catullus . . . .

So much for prose criticism. His own poetry at this period, when, be it noted, he reached full maturity, explicitly acknowledges the very same debts. *Mauberley,* for instance, is entirely built up on the basis of the "super-essential neatness," the exact-word rhyming, he treasured so highly in Gautier and in the *Pierrots* sequence of Laforgue. In the rhyming on proper names of this

>Turned from the 'eau-forte
>Par Jaquemart'
>To the strait head
>Of Messalina:

(the reference itself, indeed, is to the title page of an early edition of *Emaux et Camées*), we see mirrored his appreciation of quatrains like Gautier's

> Un vrai château d'Anne Radcliffe,
> Aux plafonds que le temps ploya,
> Aux vitraux rayés par la griffe
> Des chauves-souris de Goya....

Similarly, in the cross-language rhyming of this

> Unaffected by 'the march of events',
> He passed from men's memory in *l'an trentiesme*
> *De son eage;* the case presents
> No adjunct to the Muses' diadem.

and in the scientific terminology of this

> The face-oval beneath the glaze,
> Bright in its suave bounding-line, as
> Beneath half-watt rays,
> The eyes turn topaz.

it takes no great acumen to detect the influence of the following admired quatrain from Laforgue

> C'est, sur un cou qui, raide, émerge
> D'une frais empesée *idem*,
> Une face imberbe au cold-cream,
> Un air d'hydrocéphale asperge.

Further, in the title of the first poem of the *Mauberley* sequence— "E.P. Ode Pour L'Election de Son Sepulchre" —we have a recollection of Ronsard, and, within it, the direct quotation from Villon in the quatrain quoted above, as well as the line

> His true Penelope was Flaubert.

In a later piece he quotes from Rémy de Gourmont

> Conservatrix of Milésien,

while in the stanza

> Conduct, on the other hand, the soul
> 'Which the highest cultures have nourished'
> To Fleet St. where
> Dr. Johnson flourished.

he gives his direct recollection of Laforgue's

> Menez l'âme que les Lettres ont bien nourrie,
> Les pianos, les pianos dans les quartiers aisés!

Scarcely could a man make his debts, his homages, more explicit! In the light of these correspondences, Pound's letter to René Taupin, quoted at the outset, must be qualified indeed.

In *Propertius,* the poem in which he perfected the muscular but free, supple line that was to be his chief vehicle for the Cantos, his debt, if less obvious and less explicit (except perhaps for its *logopoeia* already referred to), is nevertheless considerable to the movement worked out by Laforgue in his *Complaints* and *Derniers Vers.* One is less able in this case to point to exact parallels (he is, after all, translating from the Latin), but I should think the similarity of movement is quite suggestive between this, from Laforgue's *Complaint Du Sage de Paris*

> Quant à *ta* mort, l'éclair aveugle en est en route
> Qui saura te choser, va, sans que tu t'en doutes.
>
> —"Il rit d'oiseaux, le pin dont *mon* cercueil viendra
> —Mais *ton* cercueil sera *ta* mort! etc . . . .

and this from *Propertius*

> . . . Yet if I postpone my obedience
>   because of this respectable terror,
> I shall be prey to lamentations worse than a
>   nocturnal assailant.
> *And* I shall be in the wrong,
>   *and* it will last a twelve month,
> For her hands have no kindness me-ward.

In sum, what he was bringing over here was the technical excellence, the crispness and hardness, the lapidary element of the best nineteenth-century French verse, in contrast to the *outrè,* grotesque, fantastical elements brought over by his predecessors. He had no ambition to *épater le bourgeois;* not, at any rate, in *their* way, which to a large extent centered around a fascinated concern with feminine nudity, not exactly with intellectual and *verbal* daring.

It should, nonetheless, be apparent that his use of these poets was mainly along the lines of *confirming* his own convictions as expressed fully for the first time in the 1910 *The Spirit of Romance;* it cannot be held that his study of these poets in any way effected in his work any essential *conversion* or *revolution*. It is only fair to Pound that we should remember this. What he found in nineteenth-century French writing was largely what he *wanted* to find: his appreciation of these poets is patently too personal in flavor for any other interpretation; we might further remember his silence on Baudelaire, Verlaine and Mallarmé. Moreover, beyond that point the direct influence of French poets—or, for that matter, of any other poets qua poets—did not advance: he has never revised these views resulting from his first study, nor have later French poets, other than Cocteau, interested him in the least. After 1920 he generates his advances wholly out of his own resources.

Behind and informing his intensely lucid interest at this period, however, stands the second aspect—a more abstract, generalized influence—which he did not by any means so consciously master and put behind him. I mean here the influence not just of French poetry, or French literature, but of French civilization, of the deeply entrenched philosophical attitudes of French culture as a whole as reflected by that literature—the French language.

I am forced to conclude that *this* influence has not proved an unmixed blessing.

For a considerable part of his career, Pound has clearly indicated his preference for French civilization as against English, particularly that civilization as it is manifested in the excessively cultivated sensibilities of a man like Rémy de Gourmont. On at least two occasions, one early, one "middle," for example, he provocatively plumps for the derivation of the name "Shakespeare" from "Jacques-pére," the implication being that a poet so capable *couldn't* have been pure Anglo-Saxon but must have been French. In the *Pisan Cantos* of 1948, probably the greatest poetry he ever wrote, again and again he comes back nostalgically to France:

> Manet painted the bar at La Cigale or at Les Folies in
>   that year
>   she did her hair in small ringlets, à la 1880 it
>   might have been,
> red, and the dress she wore Drecol or Lanvin
>   a great goddess, Aeneas knew her forthwith
> by paint immortal as no other age is immortal
>   la France dixneuvième
> Degas Manet Guys unforgettable
> a great brute sweating paint said Vanderpyl 40
>   years later of Vlaminck
> . . . .
>
>   Les moeurs passent et la douleur reste
> 'En casque de crystal rose les baladins'
>   Mallarmé, Whistler, Charles Condor, Degas
>   and the bar of the Follies
>   as Manet saw it, Degas, those two gents crossing
>   'La Concorde' or for that matter
> Judith's junk shop
>   with Théophile's arm chair
>   one cd/ live in such an apartment
>   seeing the roofs of Paris
>   Ça s'appelle une mansarde

This regard has frequently for Pound, however, a particular orientation to which I should like to draw special attention. It finds its first expression, to the best of my knowledge, as early as the 1910 *The Spirit of Romance;* note this: "Ovid—urbane, sceptical, a Roman of the city—writes, not in a florid prose, but in a verse which has the clarity of French scientific prose." The operative term is "French scientific," with its suggestion of elegant economy; note too that in 1917 he thought sufficiently of Fontenelle to translate his Dialogues into English. What I suggest is that it was above all other attractions the "scientific" character of French, its purity, clarity, neatness, irony—the formal declarative sentence brought to perfection—that gives it, for him, its peculiar fascination over English, and the peculiar fascination too of French "civilization" as he then, and apparently still, sees it. The purification and *abstraction* of language that took place in

France in the seventeenth century did not take place in any other European civilization. Which is precisely, I contend, what gives French, for Pound, its superiority.

The reason for this is undoubtedly that to a well-educated Englishman or American of the early decades of this century French civilization meant primarily the Enlightenment, Rationalism, a phase of history at that period quite uncritically revered. This oversimplification in Pound's case tied in, over-facilely no doubt, with his *literary* views on the desirability of hardness and precision in writing.

There is of course a distinction between hardness and precision in *expressing,* and hardness and precision in *judging.* Possession of the former does not automatically entail possession of the latter. From a literary standpoint we may draw attention to the great diffuseness chosen by the novelist Henry James in his late period *precisely because of* his burning need to put down exactly what he means in all its shades and gradations; something of the same may be pointed to in the case of Robert Browning, another "difficult" writer.

It has traditionally been held to represent the peculiar genius of the English tongue that it provides for the minute delineation, in every respect, of exactly what is thought; that it is, if I may so put it, "phenomenological" in nature. French, on the other hand, is aphoristic, say "positivist," turning on the "mot juste," which English *does not do*—it turns on the phrase.

Now, it happens that Pound's French studies came to a climax at the same time (World War I) as he was absorbing Fenollosa's essay on the Chinese written character and finding there what he came eventually to believe was a formulation not only of the "true" method of *phanopoeia* in poetry, but also of the true method of arriving at "true judgments" in thinking, which he, following Fenollosa, correlated with what he thought was the method of the experimental sciences—"which examined collections of fact, phenomena, specimens, and gathered general equations of real knowledge from them, even though the observed data had no syllogistic connection one with another" (*Guide to Kulchur*, 1938). This method Pound came later to epitomize famously under the deceptively Chinese characterization, the "ideogrammic method." Another gloss (this time more serviceable because less free-ranging) appears in "Canto LIX":

> periplum, not as land looks on a map
> but as sea bord seen by men sailing

How does this tie in with his French appreciations? Well, what I propose to bring out is the strict relevance of this so-called Chinese method, when applied to making judgments, rather to French Rationalism, in particular to Cartesianism.

Let me clarify. Apart from the occasional direct echoes of Descartes in the Cantos

> amo ergo sum
> and in just that proportion
> ....
> senesco sed amo

the following correspondences between Pound and Descartes can readily be noted: (1) belief in the universal validity of a method; (2) brash excursion into fields outside his own specialty; (3) break with tradition; (4) an over-facile clarity and constant insistence on same; (5) utter reliance on self, on one's own reason and intuition; (6) distrust of metaphysics and theology; (7) naive admiration for a mechanistically conceived "exact" science.

More tellingly, though, one cannot help being struck with the remarkable similarity of Jacques Maritain's epitome of Descartes' method (in *The Dream of Descartes*) to Pound's characterization of science and the ideogrammic method quoted above; says Maritain, " . . . science for Descartes develops by reducing analytically what there is to know to ideas clear and distinct in themselves, that is to say, to atoms of evidence, and by binding these atoms of evidence to one another by means of a succession of intuitions which replaces syllogism." I repeat, isn't this precisely Pound's "ideogrammic method"?

Again, in Pound's approving insistence on the strong element in French of precision, lucid intensity and clarity, haven't we an equally potentially dangerous restatement of Descartes' dictum—"I came to the conclusion that I might assume as a general rule that the things which we conceive very clearly and distinctly are all true"?

Here is one careful modern criticism of this aspect of Descartes (taken from Fr. Copleston's 1958 *History of Philosophy*):

> The clarity of Descartes is, indeed, somewhat deceptive. For it is by no means always an easy matter to interpret his meaning. And it can hardly be claimed that he is always consistent.

Again the similarity of this to the criticism applied by Noel Stock[2] to Pound's extreme reliance on unembellished "clarity" alone is striking, especially in his middle and late prose:

> If you write a sentence, caring more for 'precision' and 'concentration' than for the meaning of what you are saying, and the loose ends which in prose you must tie up, then you will arrive at such statements as, 'Not the idea but the degree of its definition determines its aptitude for reaching to music', or 'Clean the word, clearly define its borders and health pervades the whole human congeries', which look exact and profound on first reading, but begin to look ambiguous on closer examination . . . . The precision of these statements is more apparent than real.

What we have to deal with here is the conceptual, generalizing tendency of French Rationalism, embedded now in the French language itself:

> or as Jo Bard says: they never speak to each other,
> if it is baker and concierge visibly
>   it is La Rouchefoucauld and de Maintenon audibly.
>   "Canto LXXXI"

Ezra Pound, like the French Rationalists, increasingly has become committed in his methodology, which he took out-

---

[2]*Poet in Exile: Ezra Pound* (New York: Barnes & Noble, Inc., 1964).

side of poetry into the realm of "thought," not to "things" (substantial realities, essences), but to "facts," bits of evidence, *ideas*. I do not want to suggest that this orientation is in any way necessarily philosophically inferior to the English tradition of empiricism (this too only reflexively deals with "things"), but it accounts, I believe, for the strangely "foreign," alien flavor that much of Ezra Pound's poetry has for the English-speaking reader. And I suggest that in this involvement—a doctrinaire involvement—Ezra Pound has been increasingly led, in fact, not *to* but *away from* a genuine poetic "method," into disintegration and, practically, chaos.

It comes back, one supposes, to his, and our, lack of a theology backing our metaphysics and ordering our philosophies. And it is here too that so much twentieth-century poetry, largely under Pound's aegis, has come to lose significant direction. A legitimate fertile poetic technique, available for intelligent dramatic use—the juxtaposition of images and passages, without bridging matter—has been erected into an all-valid method of *ratiocination,* resulting in the glorification of irrationality and incoherence. It is a supreme misfortune that the great Pound, in the later Cantos, has been in this as much an offender as any nihilistic exhibitionist.

It is because, I feel, of Pound's eventual realization of this inner debt of his to the French language—its entrenched modalities—that in the *Pisan Cantos*, when he found it necessary to "intrude" directly into the poem his own personal emotions—that is, to *confess* his subjectivity (that is how he would see it)—he eschewed English and composed directly in French. In a dozen places, direct French phrases—and they are indeed, in their context, among the most moving he has written—are interspersed:

> Je suis au bout de mes forces/
> . . . .
> J'ai eu pitié des autres
> probablement pas assez, and at times that suited
> my own convenience
> Le paradis n'est pas artificiel,
> l'enfer non plus.

....

    repos donnez à cils
        senza termine funge   Immaculata Regina
       Les larmes que j'ai créées m'inondent
  Tard, très tard je t'ai connue, La Tristesse,
  I have been hard as youth sixty years

To reinforce this contention, I would like to quote in full, in concluding, the last great passage of verse he has written—the litany in "Canto XCIII" of *Rock Drill*, 1951:

  Lux in diafana,
           Creatrix,
                oro.
  Ursula benedetta,
             oro.
  By the hours of passion,
             per dilettevole ore,
              guide your successor,
  Ysolt, Ydone,
         have compassion,
  Picarda,
            compassion
  By the wing'd head,
        by the caduceus,
             compassion:
  By the horns of Isis-Luna,
             compassion.
  The black panther lies under his rose-tree.
  J'ai pitié des autres.
     Pas assez! Pas assez!
  For me nothing. But that the child
    walk in peace in her basilica,
  The light there almost solid.

One cannot help being forcibly struck with the fact that in this "objective" passage, while the Latin and Italian and English are used "ceremonially," the one personal phrase, at the heart of it, is in French. That language is, in fact, he has come to realize, his true natural tool.

    In the final quatrain of the superbly (on the other hand) *English* "Tudor indeed is gone" passage from the *Pisan Cantos,* he himself sums up this lifelong dialogue in language deeply suggestive of his over-personal commitment to what has been for him not a country or even a language, but essentially a *doctrine:*

> Or if a rational soul should stir, perchance,
> Within the stem or summer shoot to advance
> Contrition's utmost throw, seeking in thee
> But oblivion, not thy forgiveness, FRANCE.

A NOTE ON EZRA POUND
by Ernest Hemingway

Any poet born in this century or in the last ten years of the preceding century who can honestly say that he has not been influenced by or learned greatly from the work of Ezra Pound deserves to be pitied rather than rebuked. It is as if a prose writer born in that time should not have learned from or been influenced by James Joyce or that a traveler should pass through a great blizzard and not have felt its cold or a sand storm and not have felt the sand and the wind. The best of Pound's writing—and it is in the Cantos—will last as long as there is any literature.

November 21, 1932

Cover of Ernest Hemingway's In Our Time, *published in Paris, 1924, in a series edited by Pound.*

Hemingway by Henry Strater for In Our Time. *Strater also designed the initials for Pound's* A Draft of XVI Cantos, *Paris, 1925.*

in our time

by
ernest hemingway

> A GIRL IN CHICAGO: Tell us about the French women, Hank. What are they like?
>
> BILL SMITH: How old are the French women, Hank?

paris:
printed at the three mountains press *and for sale at* shakespeare & company, *in the rue de l'odéon;*
london: william jackson, *took's court, cursitor street, chancery lane.*

1924

Title page of In Our Time.

in our time

chapter 1

EVERYBODY was drunk. The whole battery was drunk going along the road in the dark. We were going to the Champagne. The lieutenant kept riding his horse out into the fields and saying to him, "I'm drunk, I tell you, mon vieux. Oh, I am so soused." We went along the road all night in the dark and the adjutant kept riding up alongside my kitchen and saying, "You must put it out. It is dangerous. It will be observed." We were fifty kilometers from the front but the adjutant worried about the fire in my kitchen. It was funny going along that road. That was when I was a kitchen corporal.

Opening page of In Our Time.

PIERS PLOWMAN IN THE MODERN WASTELAND

by Christine Brooke-Rose

> *nothing matters but the quality*
> *of the affection—*
> *in the end—that has carved the trace in the mind*
> *dove sta memoria*   "Canto LXXVI"

AFFECTION of the quality Pound speaks of is, like love, the dynamic element through which we see reality as constantly changing within whatever pattern our mind has had to impose on it in order to grasp it at all. This dynamism of affection is the very essence of Pound.

Of the major twentieth-century poets, Pound is at once the most purely aesthetic and the most purely didactic, an odd combination which this on the whole anti-aesthetic and anti-didactic age has found hard to swallow. And he makes the mixture even more disconcerting with a weird sense of humor, sometimes schoolboyish ("My bikini is worth your raft," says the sea nymph Leucothoe of the veil with which she saves Odysseus), sometimes uproarious in its gift for mimicry: "Noigandres!" says a great Provençal scholar in Freiburg when asked what it means,

> 'NOIgandres!
> 'You know for seex mon's of my life
> 'Effery night when I go to bett, I say to myself:
> 'Noigandres, eh, *noigandres,*
> 'Now what the DEFFIL can that mean!'
> "Canto XX"

And he often shows a comic self-awareness, not only for his own repetitions: METATHEMENON / *we are not yet out of that chapter* ("Canto LXXVII"); *Thus increasing gold imports./ The gentle reader has heard this before* ("Canto XXXVIII"); *you who think you will / get through hell in a hurry* ("Canto XLVI") but also of the very humor in his method of unexpected juxtapositions, as when, for instance, he is telling the story of Uang-iu-p'uh (a Salt Commissioner in Shensi who translated the edict of K'ang Hsi into more colloquial Chinese for the people) but never seems to get around to it:

> And that Leucothoe rose as an incense bush
> —Orchamus, Babylon—
>   resisting Apollo.
> Patience, I will come to the Commissioner
>   of the Salt Works
>   in due course . . . .   "Canto XCVIII"

These three features, aestheticism, didacticism and humor, are present throughout Pound's work, reinforcing each other as the poet and craftsman mastered the more and more recalcitrant material of his choice, which has been called many things, from simply "flux" or, in his own words, "a sufficient phalanx of particulars," to an economic history of the world. And they are held together by "the quality of the affection," which sets the Image in Action in a dynamic construction of recurrence within a constantly changing context. He himself compared the fixed symbol of the Symbolists to the numbers of arithmetic, 1, 2, 7, but the variable significance of the Image in Action to the signs a, b, x of algebra.[1]

Nothing irks him more than the static. Donald Davie

---

[1] *Gaudier-Brzeska* (London: John Lane, 1916), p. 97.

has pointed out the essential distinction made by Adrian Stokes[2] between carving—or educing from natural material qualities inherent in it (as in the best of Venice that draws the watery quality out of marble)—and molding of clay or plastics, leading to manufacture, which is an imposition of the will akin, Davie feels, to the appropriation of outside phenomena by the subjective as found in Symbolism and in the "objective correlative." Stokes goes on to equate these two activities with the male and female roles, making the further analogy of the male quarrying the mountain and the plowman's way with the land, an analogy which Pound pursues in "Canto XLVII" and relates to usura in "Canto XLVI." Or, to quote Davie:

> For, as the carver strikes the block with his chisel, so the ploughman grooves the earth—in each case to draw out of nature the wealth that lies concealed in it. On the other hand, to mold a ball of clay in the hands is to draw no wealth out of that material, but to impose the wealth of significance upon it by an act of will; and this is like giving to paper money a value that is not inherent in the paper as paper . . . . To create money out of nothing, in excess of natural wealth, to buy and sell money, to set money chasing after money, this is the way of the molder and the brickmaker, not the way of stonemason and ploughman. And this is what Pound means by 'usura'.[3]

It is this deep and affectionate concern with the living process, inherent in the very construction of the Cantos,

[2] *The Stones of Rimini* (London: Faber & Faber, Ltd., 1934). Stokes met Pound in Rapallo and Venice from 1927-29 and influenced him considerably.

[3] *Pound—Poet as Sculptor* (New York: Oxford University Press, 1964), chap. ix, p. 158. The Stokes essay was first published in the *Twentieth Century* (November, 1956). Hugh Kenner, however, holds that *all* attempts to educe stability from flux—e.g., the setting up of the dead queen Ignez de Castro (Cantos III, XXX) and *including* the "marble forest" of Venice (Venice Cantos, XXIV–XXVI, Cantos XVII, XLV) are for Pound against Nature, art defying the living process, a perversion of Nature and akin to usury ("The Broken Mirrors and the Mirror of Memory," in *Motive and Method in the Cantos of Ezra Pound*, ed. Lewis Leary [New York: Columbia University Press, 1954]) . I feel that Donald Davie's further distinction within this is more valuable as pinpointing the essential difference between Pound's attitude to external reality and that of his contemporaries.

which calls to mind a strange but illuminating parallel. For Pound has been said to languish in the shade of Eliot just as Ben Jonson, Landor and Browning languish in the shade of Shakespeare, Shelley and Tennyson. A more striking analogy, I think, is that of Langland languishing in the shade of Chaucer.[4]

To take the superficial analogy first: Like the Cantos, Langland's *Vision Concerning Piers Plowman* is a vast, apparently chaotic and plotless epic, constructed on several levels of apprehension and yielding the secrets of its organization only to those who are prepared to wrestle with them. Like the Cantos, it carries the reader along on sheer rhythm and vitality of language, whether or not he can grasp the totality. Like the Cantos it has, among the ax-grinding, passages of magnificent poetry as condensed as anything Chaucer could achieve. But a seemingly sprawling poem of great length, even when it contains exquisite passages, is unlikely to be popular. Langland has become the property of scholars passionately devoted not only to the immense textual problems but to the elucidation of the numerous quotations and topical allusions, political, social, economic and ecclesiastic. Similarly, American university departments have been busy glossing the Cantos, and if some of Pound's allusions are even more recondite than Langland's, he at least is alive to answer questions, even humorously confessing to the invention of a god the scholars had been unable to trace.

Both Pound and Langland are fundamentally moralists, both intransigent and idealistic, each hammering at what he believes to be the root of human evil, each naively reiterating that if only man could eradicate this the world would be a better place. Langland is of course primarily a medieval Christian poet concerned with salvation, but salvation as worked for in this world, in every-

---

[4] I must make it clear that by analogy I do not mean influence but a fortuitous analogy made for critical purposes. As far as I know Pound for all his extensive reading in Old and Middle English (e.g., Layamon in "Canto XCI") has never expressed any particular admiration for Langland.

day life, in politics and in the Church physical. So Pound: although his scope is wider, although he is by no means unreligious, or uninterested in the Church as an ideal political body, he is primarily concerned with *virtu,* in every conceivable sense and as worked for in every walk of life.

"What is the purpose of wealth?" asks the dreamer of Holy Church in the first vision of *Piers Plowman,* and we are reminded of *The Money Pamphlets, What is Money For?* and the insistent answers in the Cantos. As Professor Nevill Coghill has pointed out, when this question "is set in the context of Heaven and Hell, it leads beyond itself to further questions which only the Church can answer . . . . Her replies go to the roots of human need and purpose. God has given man five senses to worship Him with. As He has given these senses, so He has given their simple worldly satisfactions, namely food, drink and clothing; these may be worked for, they are the constituents of wealth; but this kind of wealth is a means and not an end . . . real wealth is of the Spirit."[5]

Holy Church's replies are not so very different from Pound's as they may seem in the medieval terminology of the poem, for in the seeking of Truth Langland moves on to the corruptions of government (very much related to the abuses of wealth), then to the sins of society and to the fear of famine: each must work in his degree to avoid starvation. "Work is honesty and that is practical Truth. Harvest will bring food for all and that is practical Love."[6] And just as Langland insists that simony and bribery are the greatest evil, so Pound hammers away at avarice and especially at usury, money made by the lending of money without goods to back it, and not from productive work. The bank of Siena (Cantos XLII-XLIV) was founded on *the abundance of nature/with the whole folk behind it* ("Canto LII"), a phrase with a truly

---

[5] Nevill Coghill, *"The Pardon of Piers Plowman"* (Gollancz Memorial Lecture, *Proceedings of the British Academy,* Vol. XXXI, 1945).

[6] *Ibid.*

Langland ring, and total order (Cantos LII-LXXI) emerges from the Li Ki, celestially, ritualistically, agriculturally, foreshadowed by the ritual passage from Hesiod in "Canto XLVII": *When the Pleiades go down to their rest, /Begin thy plowing / 40 days are they under seabord . . . ;* then the scene shifts to eighteenth-century America, where the "process" continues in Adams' actions ("Canto LXII").

Both Langland and Pound love quoting, and both love giving their sources: *as David seith in the sauter . . . ; Austyn and Ysodoros ayther of hem bothe / Nempned me thus to name . . . etc.* Similarly: *sez Orage about G.B.S. . . . ; scripsit Woodward, W.E. . . . ; (Cato speaking). . . etc.* But both are also extremely allusive. Pound quotes in many languages, assuming knowledge just as he assumes recognition of obscure historical, political, mythical and other references, sometimes purely private. So the whole of *Piers Plowman* is riddled with Latin tags and quotations, as well as political and economic allusions, some of which remind one strangely of Pound. For example, Avarice confesses:

> And with lumbarde lettres . I ladde golde to Rome,
> And take it by taille here . and tolde hem there lasse.
> (Passus V, 251-52)

From the time of Gregory IX the papacy used Italian bankers as agents for the deposit, transport and exchange of money, especially of papal dues. The bankers' representatives abroad received these from collectors and forwarded them to the Camera, for which service they got part of the money transferred, also charging for the exchange of currency. The bills of exchange were known as "letters of exchange," and the opportunities for corruption were immense. In other words, Avarice received the full amount due but when he got to Rome he counted out less. Not only do Pound's banking Cantos spring to mind *(spies and persons counterfeiting—or abetting in same—/ our continental bills of credit,* "Canto LXII"), but more specific references:

> Where the Pope goes is lack of money
> Because of the mass of clerics
>   who brings cheques for the banks to cash . . .
>   "Canto XLI"

The Jews were often known as Lombards, and Langland shows traces of anti-Semitism for much the same contextual reasons as Pound. Earlier, Avarice had said that he learned from Lombards and Jews how to clip coins on the way to the Camera (Passus V, 242-44). Again Langland refers to the Jews at Avignon in Passus XIX, alluding to the fact that the papacy's exile had brought prosperity to the Jewish community, which the Popes treated with consideration because it catered to the needs of the papal court.[7] "God amend the pope," he cries later, for he was much distressed, not only by the schism, but by the corruption it caused.

TWO

The most interesting parallel, however, between Langland and Pound is in the construction and presentation of the two poems. It is the inner poetic method in both, rather than the formal plan, which affords the real clue to the overall meaning, in spite of the fact that the formal plan in both has several layers of complexity.

The four basic keys to the Cantos are strangely similar to those which unlock *The Vision Concerning Piers Plowman*. They are: (1) the echoing orchestration, or what Hugh Kenner calls the "ground bass"; (2) the ideogrammatic method, which we may compare to Langland's constant shifting in four-level allegory; (3) the 'periplum' [sic] or voyage of discovery among facts, paralleled by Langland's weird and unconventional use of the medieval dream-formula; (4) the metamorphoses.

---

[7] Cf. Del Mar's interesting and sympathetic lecture on "Usury and the Jews," delivered to the Young Men's Hebrew Association of San Francisco in 1879, which received great applause, and in which he shows how the Church and early Christian monarchs, by closing all other trades to the Jews, forced them into usury because, though forbidden, it was useful to them. Del Mar is one of Pound's main sources on the history and nature of money.

Rather than analyze these comparatively one by one, I shall try to summarize Langland's great poem, which, like the Cantos but more so for reasons of language, remains unfamiliar except in selected extracts. And I shall do so in terms of the first three basic keys enumerated above as used by Langland: the echoing orchestration; the constant shift in four-level allegory; the unconventional use of the medieval dream-formula.[8] I shall then be able to deal with the metamorphoses in the light of this description.

The Vision Concerning Piers Plowman is formally divided into two main parts, the *Visio* (Prologue to Passus VII) and the *Vita* (Passus VIII–XX). In the *Visio* (the World of Affairs), the author falls asleep and dreams he is in the "field full of folk" (pilgrims, palmers, merchants, minstrels, pardoners, beggars, knaves and priests, a king and his knights, etc.). A lady comes down from a tower and speaks to him; she is Holy Church, and she says that Love is the readiest way to Heaven, and Truth is the best of all treasures. He asks how he can know Falsehood and she bids him turn to see him.

Then follows one of the most fantastic *danses macabres* in literature, in which allegorical figures mingle with real people and become flesh and blood: the Lady Meed, Simony, Civil, Theology, Conscience, Reason and many others have strange adventures with merchants, pardoners, friars, judges, and the king himself. There is a mad ride to London (for which sheriffs, assizers, summoners and deans are saddled as horses to carry Meed, Falsehood, Flattery, etc.) to see the king about the quarrel as to whether Meed (whose name means both bribery and reward) should marry Falsehood or Truth; Dread was at the door, and heard the judgment, and bade Falsehood flee, Liar leapt through the bylanes, nowhere welcome, but pardoners took him in, leeches (physicians) invited

---

[8] The medieval dream-formula is in fact usually combined with allegory, nearly always a simple two-level allegory. The poet or protagonist falls asleep and in his dream a personage speaks to him, either a dead loved person (as in Dante, or *The Pearl*) or allegorical characters representing sentiments, virtues, vices and psychological realities *(Le Roman de la Rose).*

him, spicers asked him to be their shopkeeper and finally the Friars fetched him in and clothed him as a friar. The dreamer wakes and passes into the next dream. We are back in the Field of Folk, which has a different aspect, that of the World of Contrition. Conscience is hearing the confessions of the Seven Deadly Sins. Hope seizes a horn, thousands of pilgrims throng to find Truth. Piers Plowman enters and says he knows Truth well, he has sown his seed and he will guide them, but first he must plow his half-acre and they must help him. More adventures follow, with Hunger and Waster sabotaging the labor. Truth bids Piers work before the famine comes, and promises a pardon to all who help him. A priest asks to see the pardon, which says *Et qui bona egerunt, ibunt in vitam eternam* . . ., and he declares it is no pardon at all. Piers tears it up in mortification. The dreamer wakes and muses on the meaning of the pardon: those that do well . . .

The *Vita* is a long sequence of more dreams, the author's quest, through more weird adventures among men and ideas, for *Do-Well* or the World of Moral Interpretation (VII-XV), *Do-Bet* or the Priestly Life (XVI-XVIII) and *Do-Best* or the Episcopal Life (XIX-XX).

The plan thus simplified sounds schematic enough, but the execution is more akin to surrealism than to moral allegory. Dream follows dream with no schematism at all, ungainly abstractions become flesh and blood and mingle with human beings very much on their own often sordid level: the Seven Deadly Sins, for instance, confess as if they were the sinners not the sins, and they are in fact completely humanized; the people try to poison Hunger by feeding him, food being the death of hunger. Piers Plowman appears and disappears at the oddest moments, in new guises: first as an honest farmer, servant of Truth, a married man, humble and hard-working and obedient to the Church (portrait of Do-Well); later he is the man who can tell the nature of the Tree of Charity, who can expound the mystery of the Trinity, he is the Good Samaritan, he is Christ, he has the added virtues of teaching, healing and suffering (portrait of Do-Bet); next he is entrusted with the building of the Church of Christ, he is Peter, yet an ordinary plowman again (Grace makes Piers his plowman) with a job to do, Piers the Builder of the Barn (portrait of Do-Best); finally he vanishes altogether, after the wild confusion in the last Passus, with Anti-Christ overturning Truth and dashing kings and popes to dust, and Conscience declares that he will turn pilgrim and seek Piers Plowman.

The dream-like quality of the poem masks the didacticism. Abraham and Moses wander in and out as Faith and Hope. The dreamer is more and more puzzled. By the end of the Do-Well section he is still wondering what Do-Well means. It is one of the fundamental difficulties of *Piers Plowman,* but also its greatest charm, that there is no clear division between Do-Well, Do-Bet and Do-Best. They are all three introduced early in the Do-Well section, indeed by implication in the *Visio,* and continue throughout, precisely because the second and third are constant ideals while practicing the first. After a long passage about charity, when the dreamer is told that Charity is God's champion and only Piers knows him, the dreamer says thank you, but what is Charity? It is a fruit on the tree of Patience, which grows in the heart, the land belonging to Piers Plowman. In Passus XVIII, a beautiful passage describes the author wandering wearily and falling asleep again; he dreams it is Palm Sunday and sees the Good Samaritan ride forth, but he cannot quite distinguish him, he looks like Piers Plowman; Faith (Abraham) proclaims the son of David and says that Christ is coming to joust in Piers's armor against the fiend. The Crucifixion follows, vividly described in a swift, breathless style: the two thieves are there with broken legs; a blind knight jousts with Jesus and pierces his heart, but is healed of his blindness; at night the dead bodies rise from the graves; then from West and East come Mercy and Truth, and from North and South come Righteousness and Peace. What was lost by a tree is won back by a tree, death shall destroy death, says Mercy, but Truth, in a curious way, refuses to believe it.

The frequent puzzlement of even the chief protagonists,

In preparing his typescript for A Draft of XVI Cantos *(Paris, 1925), Pound made use of Cantos already published in* Dial. *These four introductory lines, added to pages of the Canto torn from the* Dial *of May, 1922, became "Canto II."*

2 lines on 20 cie -
" " 25
6 " "
rest on 35

II

H

Hang it all, Robert Browning,
there can be but the one "Sordello";
So-shu churned in the sea
And the wave runs in the beach-groove:

"*The Eighth Canto*," from Dial, *as corrected to become part of* "*Canto II.*"

EIGHTH CANTO

BY EZRA POUND

Dido choked up with tears for dead Sichaeus;
And the weeping Muse, weeping, widowed, and willing
The weeping Muse
        Mourns Homer,
Mourns the days of long song,
Mourns for the breath of the singers,
Winds stretching out, seas pulling to eastward,
Heaving breath of the oarsmen,
        triremes under Cyprus,
The long course of the seas,
The words woven in wind-wrack,
        salt spray over voices.
Tyro to shoreward lies lithe with Neptunus
And the glass-clear wave arches over them;
Seal sports in the spray-whited circles of cliff-wash,
Sleek head, daughter of Lir,
        eyes of Picasso
Under black fur-hood, lithe daughter of Ocean;
And the wave runs in the beach-groove:
"Eleanor, ἑλέναυς and ἑλέπτολις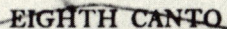
    And poor old Homer blind, blind, as a bat,
Ear, ear for the sea-surge, murmur of old men's voices:
"Let her go back to the ships,
Back among Grecian faces,
        lest evil come on our own,
Evil and further evil, and a curse cursed on our children.
Moves, yes she moves like a goddess
And has the face of a god
        and the voice of Schoeney's daughters,
And doom goes with her in walking,
Let her go back to the ships,
        back among Grecian voices."

Page-proof additions by the author, "Canto II," Paris edition of 1925.

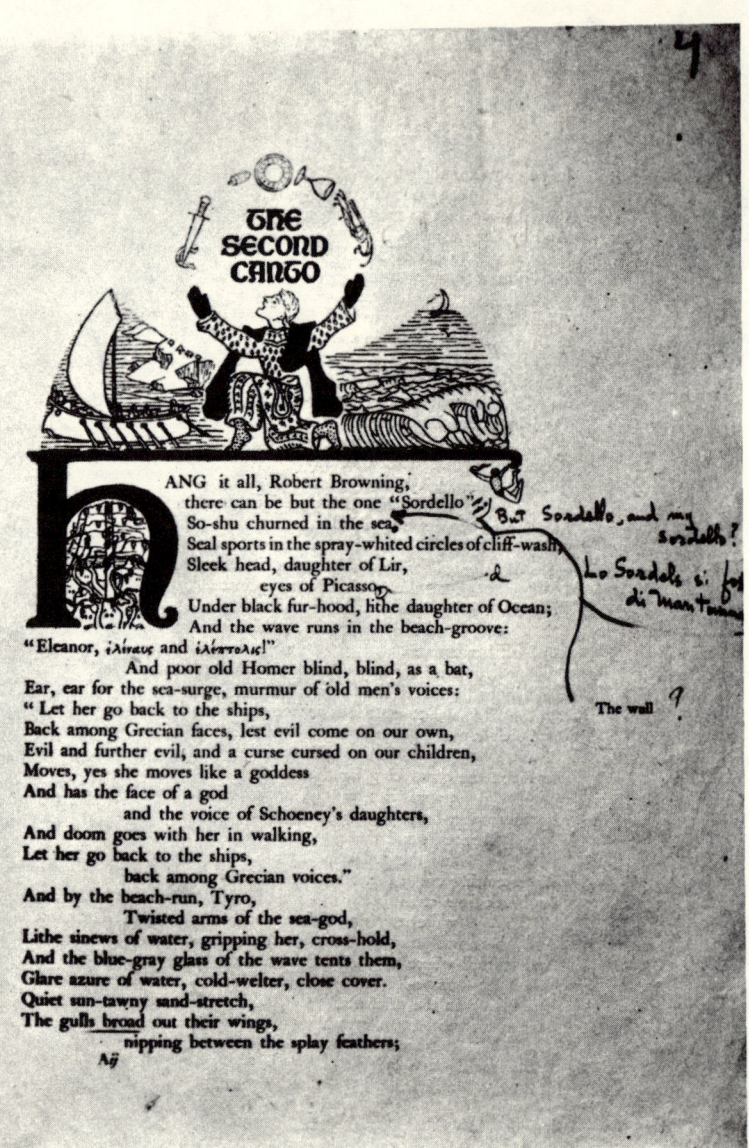

THE SECOND CANTO

HANG it all, Robert Browning,
there can be but the one "Sordello."
So-shu churned in the sea.
Seal sports in the spray-whited circles of cliff-wash,
Sleek head, daughter of Lir,
    eyes of Picasso
Under black fur-hood, lithe daughter of Ocean;
And the wave runs in the beach-groove:
"Eleanor, ἑλέναυς and ἑλέπτολις!"
    And poor old Homer blind, blind, as a bat,
Ear, ear for the sea-surge, murmur of old men's voices:
" Let her go back to the ships,
Back among Grecian faces, lest evil come on our own,
Evil and further evil, and a curse cursed on our children,
Moves, yes she moves like a goddess
And has the face of a god
    and the voice of Schoeney's daughters,
And doom goes with her in walking,
Let her go back to the ships,
    back among Grecian voices."
And by the beach-run, Tyro,
    Twisted arms of the sea-god,
Lithe sinews of water, gripping her, cross-hold,
And the blue-gray glass of the wave tents them,
Glare azure of water, cold-welter, close cover.
Quiet sun-tawny sand-stretch,
The gulls broad out their wings,
    nipping between the splay feathers;

[margin notes: "But Sordello, and my Sordello? / Lo Sordels si fo di Mantoana"; "The wall?"]

from Piers to Truth himself, increases the dreamy effect which blurs not only the formal plan and the didacticism, but also the allegorical schematism. Professor Coghill has most succinctly brought out the four levels of allegory (literal, moral, allegorical and anagogical, as described in Dante's *Convivio* and ultimately deriving from Origen's threefold system) in *Piers Plowman:*

Sensus literalis	*S. allegoricus*	*S. moralis*	*S. anagogicus*
Piers the Farmer	The Laity	Do-Well	God the Father
Piers the Teacher, Healer and Sufferer	The Clergy	Do-Bet	God the Son
Piers the Builder of the Barn	The Episcopacy	Do-Best	God the Holy Ghost

All this is there, but it does not explain the structure of the poem, because, unlike much medieval allegory (which is, mostly, on two levels only, literal and moral), it is not mechanically applied. Langland's achievement is to make us pass from one level to another without realizing it, indeed, to make us apprehend all levels at once. There are no placards saying: "You are now entering the anagogic zone."

Perhaps the easiest way to understand the structure of *Piers Plowman* is to think of it as a spiral, with the Field of Folk in the center. On one side of the field is the Dungeon and Satan's Castle of Care, on the other the Tower of Truth. As we go up the spiral on higher and higher levels we go through Evil on one side and Good on the other. The Field of Folk recurs at each level with enriched meanings, as a sinful, muddled place, as a place of contrition, as Piers Plowman's half-acre, as various kinds of *activa vita* throughout Part II (the *Vita*), as the heart where grows the Tree of Patience (the land belonging to Piers Plowman), as the place of the Crucifixion, as the field where the Barn is being built, as the battleground of Anti-Christ. Motifs recur on new levels: the Seven Deadly Sins implicitly throughout and explicitly again in Passus XIV; the good Samaritan dream in Passus XVIII echoes Passus XVII, in which he is seen coming across the wounded man who was going to Jericho (i.e., he himself must have been going to Jerusalem, and the next scene is in fact the Crucifixion), Faith and Hope (Abraham and Moses) having passed the robbed man but the Samaritan alighting. People and allegorical figures move in and out, reiterating things with new significance. The theme of the Incarnation and Crucifixion is echoed and re-echoed throughout as the very centerpiece of the Field of Folk or *Activa Vita,* even from the very beginning, when Truth says of Love that Heaven could not hold it, it was so heavy of itself, until it had eaten its fill of earth, when it became lighter than a linden leaf (Passus I, quoted in Middle English on p. 176); or again in Passus V, after the confessions of the Deadly Sins:

> But in owre secte [suit, flesh] was the sorwe and thi sone it ladde,
> *Captivam duxit captivitatem.*
> the sonne for sorwe ther-of . les sy3te [saw less] for a tyme
> Aboute mydday, whan most li3te is . and mele-tyme [mealtime] of seintes;
> Feddest with thi fresche blode . owre forfadres in derknesse,
> *Populus qui ambulabat in tenebris, vidit lucem magnam;*
> And thorw the li3te that lepe oute of the . lucifer was blent [blinded],
> And blewe alle thi blissed . into the blisse of paradise.
>
> (498-503)

THREE

It is this system of foretastes and echoes which most reminds us of Pound's Cantos. He has himself described them as "an epic poem which begins 'In the Dark Forest,' crosses the Purgatory of human error, and ends in the light."[9] It is certainly possible to think of Cantos I–XXX as Hell; of Cantos XXXI-XLI (Jefferson-Nuevo Mundo), the 5th Decad (Siena-Leopoldine Reforms) and LII–LXXI (the Chinese dynasties and back to Adams in action) as Purga-

---

[9] *"An Introduction to the Economic Nature of the United States" (Money Pamphlets* by £, No. 1, London, 1950).

tory, with the synthesis of the *Pisan Cantos* (LXXIV–LXXXI) as a personal Purgatory; *Rock Drill* (LXXXV–XCV) and *Thrones* (XCVI–CIX), which are flooded with light, as Paradise.

But Hell, Purgatory and Paradise are constantly superimposed on one another throughout. Even in the actual "Hell Cantos" (XIV–XVI) the purgators appear (Blake, Dante, Augustine) and the Elysium Fields of earned paradise. The descent to Tiresias of "Canto I" is echoed in the opening of "Canto XLVII" (*Who even dead, yet hath his mind entire! / This sound came in the dark / First must thou go the road / to hell*), and again in "Canto LXXX." Both Hell and Paradise, as well as the Purgatory of *Activa Vita,* reverberate in the *Pisan Cantos* and in *Rock Drill: Le paradis n'est pas artificiel, / l'enfer non plus* ("Canto LXXVI"), echoed from "Canto LXXIV," and again in *Rock Drill: Le Paradis n'est pas artificiel / but is jagged, / For a flash, / for an hour./ Then agony* ("Canto XCII"); *"Oh you", as Dante says / "in the dinghy astern there"* ("Canto XCIII") echoed again as the very last line of *Thrones: You in the dinghey (piccioletta) astern there!* ("Canto CIX"). On a more personal note, the *Pisan Cantos* can juxtapose the peace of this passage:

> To study with the white wings of time passing
>   is not that our delight
> to have friends come from far countries
>   is not that pleasure
> nor to care that we are untrumpeted?

with the almost infernal despair of:

> is there a blacker or was it merely San Juan with a belly
>   ache
>   writing ad posteros
> in short shall we look for a deeper or is this the bottom?
>   "Canto LXXIV"

I have called *Piers Plowman* a spiral. Two of the most important concepts in Pound's prose criticism are the Vortex (which became an artistic movement) and the Unwobbling Pivot (Confucius) in life's centripetal chaos. *The*

Waste Land, which may be called the Cantos in miniature, is like a small spiral staircase in a narrow tower, in which reverberate the echoes not only of past cultures, but of other passages in the poem itself. The Cantos are a giant spiral, in a huge tower, with a vast and complex field of *activa vita* in the center. Each time a phrase or image recurs, we are at a different level in the spiral so that the changed context of *activa vita* gives it, as in *Piers Plowman*, new reverberations of meaning, and so a new interpretation in the organic whole.[10] *Thrones* is at the top of this huge tower, *Rock Drill*[11] having pierced through the rock roof, with the spiral narrower and narrower and the echoes more and more frequent, allusive, numerous, richer and richer in associations and with more and more startling juxtapositions.

FOUR

It is the unexpectedness which, as in *Piers Plowman*, is so exciting and yet makes the poem so difficult. Pound's method has been called ideogrammatic. The Chinese ideogram juxtaposes various signs for facts or concepts to make a new fact or concept. One may of course argue that these separate elements are not alive in the mind every time the ideogram is used, any more than the old etymologies are

[10] This concept of the spiral is a peculiarly modern scientific concept for a man who, as Noel Stock has shown *(Poet in Exile* [New York: Barnes & Noble, Inc., 1964], chap. xv), otherwise had a naively mechanistic, nineteenth-century idea of science. I develop this further in an essay on the so-called "Two Cultures" ("Dynamic Gradients," *London Magazine,* March, 1965)), with reference to Pound, Virginia Woolf and three modern experimental novelists, Nathalie Sarraute, Alain Robbe-Grillet and Samuel Beckett.

[11] Named after Epstein's sculpture, executed in plaster in 1913, exhibited in London in 1916, of a man drilling. Epstein used a real drill and thought of attaching pneumatic power to it and setting it in motion, "thus completing every potentiality of form and movement in one single work." He later decided against it, and only the upper part of the figure was cast in gunmetal. (Jacob Epstein, *Epstein: An Autobiography* [New York: E. P. Dutton & Co., 1963]). See also Robert Black, *The Art of Jacob Epstein* (London, 1942); B. Van Dieren, *Epstein* (1920), p. 50; Pound's chapter on Epstein in *Gaudier-Brzeska* and his estimate for the *Egoist,* March 16, 1914; and T. E. Hulme's description of the Rock Drill drawing in the *New Age,* December 25, 1913.

alive in each component of every word we use, but the job of the poet, with both the word and the image, is to Make It New, and Pound does this by the ideogrammatic method of juxtaposition. The technique is crucial to the Cantos, which form a continuous asyndeton in the juxtaposition of apparently disparate facts, often jumbled in time, like a giant agglutinative metaphor extending itself not only for a passage but for a whole Canto, indeed for the whole poem.

The "Mitteleuropa Canto," for example (XXXV), and the "Canzone d'Amore" (XXXVI) are not only juxtaposed to each other but are placed in the middle of the Jefferson Cantos, the moral chaos of Europe counterpointing the ideals of eighteenth-century America, and perfect love counterpointing Europe's moral chaos. Similarly, the leap from Nuevo Mundo (XXXI–XXXVIII) to Mussolini (XLI) is offset by the Fertility Rites and Circe (men into swine) of "Canto XXXIX" and by the *periplous* (circumnavigation) through the press and commercial squalor of "Canto XL," each of these foiling the other and each full of further juxtapositions within (e.g., the *periplous* through the press and Hanno's voyage of discovery). If Langland does not put up placards to announce a new level of allegory, neither does Pound stop to explain why he leaps from Confucius to John Adams in action, or from Odysseus (in one sentence) to Guillaume of Aquitaine, or from Yeats and Arthur Symons to *Kuthera deina*, Boticelli, Chu Hsi and Malatesta; we simply leap with him. As Professor Coghill has said, the gift of transferred and simultaneous thinking on several levels has something of the quality of metaphor (the union of similarity and dissimilarity—and what could be more dissimilar, in the allegorical schema, than the laity and God the Father?). It is a gift which we have largely lost since the Middle Ages, and which Pound has done much to restore to us.

FIVE

Facts, facts, facts—historical, cultural, social, political, agricultural, economic, private, mythical. Pound juxtaposes them endlessly as moving images, links them with echoes reverberating down the vortex of his poem, a *sufficient phalanx of particulars*. He sees himself as an Odysseus *polumetis*, on a voyage of discovery—the *periplous*—through facts. So Langland passes from one dream to another through the succession of varyingly weird representations of *activa vita*. The dream-formula is his *periplous,* Pound's *periplous* is "the mirror of memory." Both poems are full of people —fictional, historical or allegorical in Langland, fictional, historical or mythical in Pound. And in both poems they are constantly changing their nature or changing into one another.

Pound is obsessed with metamorphoses. This aspect of the Cantos has been so clearly dealt with by critics[12] that I shall do no more than summarize it and point out the analogy. It is not only the "throwing aside of mask after mask" (T. S. Eliot, *Athenaeum*, 1919), but, as D. S. Carne-Ross has pointed out, "it is a basic principle of *The Cantos* that all related characters can merge or meet, into one another."[13] *Let us consider the osmosis of persons,* says Pound in "Canto XXIX," but he starts doing so much earlier. Cantos II–VII deal with passion myths, modes of love and violence in metamorphosis. The Helen theme (Danae, Eleanor of Aquitaine and others) is counterpointed throughout by the Cunizza theme (fidelity, Proene, Cabestan's lady and others), while various women whose flesh enshrined the ideal of eternal beauty merge into one another, as do gods and goddesses. His villains recur as archetypes of one another, as do his heroes. We are reminded of Langland's strange allegorical figures, whose very natures change in contact with different human beings or different qualities (Lady Meed being both bribery and reward, hence her marriage either to Truth or Falsehood); or of Faith turning

---

[12] See especially "The Metamorphoses of Ezra Pound," by Sister M. Bernetta Quinn, O.S.F., in *Motive and Method in the Cantos of Ezra Pound.*

[13] *An Examination of Ezra Pound,* ed. Peter Russell (Norfolk, Conn.: New Directions, 1950), and under the title *Ezra Pound* (London, 1950).

into Abraham, and of the metamorphoses of Piers himself.

But it is not only the people who change. Pound has said in *Affirmations:* "The undeniable tradition of metamorphosis teaches us that things do not remain the same. They become other things by swift and unanalysable process." Pomona (she was wooed by Vertumnus, whose name means "he who changes") recurs regularly to represent the cycle of the year, as does Atthis, whose spirit passed into the tree under which he died, flowers springing from his blood. The Cadmus story echoes in Cantos XXVII, XXXIII, LXII, LXXVII and CII, and the metamorphoses of rocks, the decomposition of the body and descent into plant life are dealt with in Cantos XXVII, XXXVII and LXXX. More important still is the metamorphic treatment of ideas. Apart from the explicit indictment against Usura in the two notorious "Usura Cantos," Pound uses two major stories of transformation in order to "make new" the idea that it is vicious to twist the will as usury does (the will is also strongly present in Langland, and the author-dreamer's name Long Will may be a pun): the story of Circe and the swine, and the Bacchus-Acoetes myth (the sailors change course to sell the god in Egypt and are therefore punished); as well as minor stories such as that of Midas. Similarly, the idea that beauty is very hard to possess (*So very difficult, Yeats, beauty so difficult,* "Canto LXXX") is treated in terms of metamorphosis stories (Danae, Acteon, Salmacis, Piere Vidal disguised as a wolf).

The whole structure of the Cantos is one of constant metamorphosis, as is that of *Piers Plowman,* through the not so dissimilar method of the allegorical dream-vision. Yeats, in *A Packet for Ezra Pound,* tells us how this metamorphic principle was to be applied in the new epic: Pound explained that he would use the descent into hell as one theme (ABCD), and metamorphosis as a second (JKLM); that he would repeat these, inverting and repeating the first (DCBA) to fit the changing circumstances; that he would introduce archetypal persons (XYZ) and a fifth element, symbolized by any letters that never recur, to stand for contemporary events; finally setting all sorts of combinations of ABCD, JKLM, XYZ, DCBA whirling together.[14]

SIX

Whirling is just about the right word: like the spiral construction of *Piers Plowman,* in the center of which lies the Field of Folk, or, in Pound, the modern wasteland, seen each time from a new vantage point. But the *Piers Plowman* spiral, with its *activa vita* in the center, seems to get wider and wider, like a vast megaphone put out from earth to Heaven, whereas Pound's tower is conical, so that the circling gets smaller and smaller, and the views of humanity at the center, though in some ways of wider reference, change more and more swiftly, the echoes from below become more and more frequent, more and more resonant.

It is true that the Cantos are very much more allusive and difficult than *The Vision Concerning Piers Plowman.* Langland, for all his learning, was more widely understood in his day than Pound is now; Pound's references, usually esoteric and often private, assume much more knowledge than Langland's would have assumed in his own time, though it could be argued that their presence in the Cantos may crystallize knowledge or information that would otherwise have vanished or been hard to come by. Langland is also more inventive: the metamorphoses, allegories and adventures are all his own, whereas Pound's myths and much of his material (translations, letters and documents) are ready-made and what matters is the manner of presentation. Langland, moreover, passes from one level to another with metaphor as well as with racing narrative. Pound rarely uses metaphor, and his facts are simply put down one after the other asyndetically. Yet his acute sense of the unusual but right word—*le mot juste*—his wit and humor, his versatile but usually free and basically trochaic rhythm *(to break the pentameter, that was the first heave,* "Canto LXXXI"; *and as for those who deform thought with*

[14] Dublin: Cuala Press, 1929.

iambics, "Canto XCVIII") sweep up over such objections much as Langland's swift alliterative meter, richness of language and humorous dramatic presentation sweep us through the didacticism and the oddity of what his people say and do.

What is it that emerges most vividly from these two giant whirls? Perhaps each poet's extraordinary inclusiveness, an essentially medieval quality, born of the desire not only to assimilate the whole of reality but to interconnect all its multiple and changing aspects. And always love is the linking power, the "quality of the affection," beyond the anger and the didacticism:

What thou lovest well remains,
         the rest is dross
What thou lovest well shall not be reft from thee . . .

The ant's a centaur in his dragon world.
Pull down thy vanity, it is not man
Made courage, or made order, or made grace,
 Pull down thy vanity, I say pull down.
Learn of the green world what can be thy place
In scaled invention or true artistry . . .
         "Canto LXXXI"

Fisshe to lyve in the flode . and in the fyre the crykat,
The corlue by kynde of the eyre . most clennest fflessh of bryddes,
And bestes by grasse and by greyne . and by grene rotis,
In menynge that alle men . my3te the same
Lyve thorw lele byleve . and love, as god witnesseth.
         (Passus XIV)

Or love descending (Cavalcanti's *Canzone d' Amore*):

Never adorned with rest Moveth he changing colour
Either to laugh or weep
Contorting the face with fear
 resteth but a little
Yet shall ye see of him That he is most often
With folk who deserve him . . .
         "Canto XXXVI"

And of love, less catharistically, being fulfilled by the descent:

> For hevene my3te nou3te holden it . it was so hevy
>   of hym-self,
> Tyl it hadde of the erthe . yeten his fylle.
> And whan it haved of this folde . flesshe and blode taken,
> Was nevere leef upon lynde. ly3ter ther-after,
> And portatyf and persant . as the poynt'of a nedle,
> That my3te non armure it lette . ne none hei3 walles.
>
> (Passus I)

The difficulty of Pound's method does however remain a stumbling block to many. Even in his prose Pound presents his ideas, not discursively but ideogrammatically, and his view of history and the high achievements of past civilizations is idiosyncratic and highly selective. This is what gives his poetry a disturbingly apocalyptic quality very akin to Langland's. Just as in his early translations he made "howlers" but, uncannily, despite and even sometimes through them, got at the spirit of the original, whereas some of his later translations are less good in this way, so one often feels, when reading even the most didactic passages in the Cantos, that he may in a very ultimate sense be right, as only a poet can be both right and wrong at the same time. Even on the question of economics, the present order may not last for ever, any more than feudalism did.

In the end, though, it is not even his ideas that matter, but the "ideas in action," that is to say, the poetry itself. The Cantos are difficult, but very rewarding, especially for those who are prepared to go some way with the poet, follow him to his sources (which he usually gives) and see what he does with them. Above all, the Cantos represent a lifetime of reading, loving, suffering, and a lifetime of patient craftsmanship, an *activa vita*. And as Pound himself says in *Thrones, There is no substitute for a lifetime*.

THE FENOLLOSA PAPERS

Ernest Fenollosa went from Harvard to a teaching post in Japan, before the turn of the century. He became an authority on Japanese art and was appointed Imperial Commissioner of Art. Before his death in 1908 he studied Chinese poetry under Japanese scholars.

Mrs. Fenollosa, after seeing some of Ezra Pound's verse in Poetry, *decided he was the person best fitted to take charge of her husband's literary remains and handed them over to him, in London, toward the end of 1913. They included Fenollosa's jottings and notebooks on Chinese poetry. What Pound made of this material we know from* Cathay. *But what the material looked like before Pound went to work on it is scarcely known at all. It is fitting therefore that we give a page from one of the Fenollosa notebooks and opposite it one of the finished poems from* Cathay, *on the following two pages.*

Sei blue	*Sei* blue	*Ka* river	*han* bank side	*So* grass
utsu luxuriantly spread the willow	*utsu* luxuriantly spread the willow	*en* garden	*chu* in	*rin* willow
yei face full the full bloom of youth	*yei* face full the full bloom of youth	*so* storied house	*jo* on	*jo* girl
Ko white brilliant luminous	*Ko* white brilliant luminous	*to* just face	*So* window	*yo* door
Ga beauty of face	*ga* beauty of face	*Ko* red (of berri)	*fun* powder	*So* toilet
Sen slender	*Sen* slender	*Shutsu* put forth	*so* white blank not dyed	*Shu* hand
Seki in former times	*i* was (did)	*Sho* courtesan	*Ka* house	*jo* girl
Kon now	*i* is	*to* dissipated	*Shi* son's	*fu* wife
To dissipated	*Shi* son	*Ko* go away	*fu* not	*Ki* return
Ku empty	*Sho* bed	*nan* hard	*doku* only one alone	*shu* keep

The Beautiful Toilet

Blue, blue is the grass about the river
And the willows have overfilled the close garden.
And within, the mistress, in the midmost of her
    youth,
White, white of face, hesitates, passing the door.
Slender, she puts forth a slender hand,

And she was a courtezan in the old days,
And she has married a sot,
Who now goes drunkenly out
And leaves her too much alone.

by Mei Sheng, B. C. *140*

The poet with his father, Homer Pound, on Lake Garda, with Sirmione in the background.

Pound with his granddaughter Patrizia and grandson Walter, at Brunnenburg, after his return to Italy, 1958.

AN APPRECIATION

by Tom Scott

Ezra Pound's eightieth birthday is a good time to try to pull together some of one's impressions of his work and achievement. I shall concern myself almost entirely here with the credit side, as I see it, since a birthday party is not the time for a guest to discuss his host's shortcomings; and even a perfectionist, perhaps especially a perfectionist, has his shortcomings.

Firstly, there is the much-witnessed fact of his wide promotion of other men's work—Joyce, Hemingway, Eliot, Gaudier-Brzeska, Cocteau and dozens of other poets, writers, artists, musicians; his promotion of magazines, finding of patrons, editing of anthologies, persuasion of publishers. The generosity of this self-imposed labor in itself is a great merit; the critical fact that he rarely picked a dud, that he, in his own phrase, "delivered the goods," argues critical genius in the very young man who had this unerring perception and the conviction to fight for his own choices. Mr. Ronald Duncan has written of the one-man university Pound made of himself for young poets, and there is plenty of other evidence of this willingness to spend himself and his on the young. One of the romantic lies which is still with us is that poetry cannot be taught. It can, it has been, it is and it will be. This does not apply of course to inspiration, but if a man has not learned his job, he will either get no inspiration or be unable to use it when it comes—he will merely suffer an inexpressible state of emotional possession, waste of energy. An engineer may have inspiration as well as a poet, but if he doesn't know his job as an engineer, the divinity has breathed in vain. All that a man can do unaided can be taught, can be learned, and must be. This is particularly true of poets, who had, in the great days of bardship, the most exacting schools, the most rigorous and lengthy training, the most severe disciplines to undergo throughout their lives. Yet today poets, so-called, think to earn the favors of the Muse with less effort than the average professional musician, painter or actor or whatever would consider minimal. This is partly due to a bad academic tradition; for, whereas the training of a student at a musical academy or an art school or a college of drama is intensely practical, aimed at turning out executants, not commentators, our literary schools at universities so operate that a student can do a four-year honors course in literature, come out at the end of it "authorized" to blather endlessly on or off a rostrum "about" literature, and be totally unable to write a sestina, a canzone, a villanelle, a ballade, much less a narrative poem, epic, drama, or even a short story or a novel —anything, in fact, except a short "critical" essay. And what can a man know about an art if he hasn't practiced it? Pound, in making a one-man university of himself, was not merely indulging his ego, his personal vanity; he was recognizing and trying to fulfill a much-felt need. This is entirely to his credit, and the need has been recognized, and to some extent met, by many other significant (i.e., *good*) poets of our time; most notably, by Robert Graves, T. S. Eliot, Herbert Read and some Americans. Pound, like every poet who *is* a poet, has always known that there is no art of poetry without the craft of verse, and that the craft of verse can be taught, can be learned.

Pound's qualifications for this tutorial side of his work are incomparable, and bring me to his poetic achievement itself. I cannot itemize the whole of this achievement here, even if I knew it all, and I don't. But some things are obvious: his early work brought into English a new cadence and rhythm, a new elegance and freedom within the law, a new fineness and sensitivity. For instance, his early "Speech for Psyche in the Golden Book of Apuleius":

> All night, and as the wind lieth among
> The cypress trees, he lay,
> Nor held me save as air that brusheth by one
> Close, and as the petals of flowers in falling
> Waver and seem not drawn to earth, so he
> Seemed over me to hover light as leaves
> And closer me than air,
> And music flowing through me seemed to open
> Mine eyes upon new colours.
> O winds, what wind can match the weight of him!

That poem catches, as no previous one in English has done, the very movement and texture of a light, warm breeze; and this is one way of trying to imagine Psyche's experience of Eros, the secret and invisible god who came to her in a swirl of air in the covering dark. That one poem, from his first volume, is enough to announce the presence of a revolutionary new poet. I say "revolutionary" advisedly, because it is the last word many would apply to Pound. Even his use of apparent "archaisms" here, and throughout his work (e.g., the "eth" endings, the use of "mine" possessively), is a revolutionary use. He gets rid of the "hissing geese" of s's, promotes euphony, cuts out hindering auxiliaries— and pays his price for it among the less alert. Yes, there is the whiff of the ink pot; but literature is by definition not oral, and no considerable poet can confine himself only to the spoken usage of his time. Pound's usage, here and elsewhere, is a cleansing and purifying of the instrument, never a mere nostalgia. San Juan de la Cruz has written an even more wonderful ethereal poetry than the above, in his "En una noce oscura," but not in English.

That one poem is enough, but abundance is added to sufficiency in that first volume: "Cino," "De Aegypto," "Night Litany," "Altaforte," "Francesca," "Ballatetta," "Erat Hora," "The Flame"—each adds its own innovation, however slight, to the technique of English verse; they were all published before Pound was twenty-five. For sheer grace of melody there had been nothing like them since Campion—and they are a technical advance on his work. This sense of melody, one remembers, was correctly defined by Coleridge as the hallmark of the true poet.

Pound himself has spoken of three aspects of poetic technique: melody (melopoeia); image (phanopoeia); and "the dance of intellect among words" (logopoeia). In the volumes from 1912 up to *Mauberley* (1920) these three strands are further developed, separately, and blended together in a new, highly sensitive and unique verse-instrument. The famous "Seafarer" version was a necessary development: the delicate melodic line, having been spun out, had to be deepened and broadened without losing its essential quality, and the remaking of "The Seafarer" did just this. It is not a "translation," of course, if one sticks to Dryden's excellent differentia, in the sense of "metaphrase." That can best be done by scholars, in prose, aiming at exactness, and with no creative purpose whatsoever. Pound is not a "translator" at all, in this sense. The object of the exercise he sets himself in his "paraphrases" (again to use Dryden's term) is not "translation" but versification, i.e., the creation of a new poem out of the old. To fail to grasp this is to misunderstand him as he has been misunderstood. What matters, as Eliot pointed out in his remarks on *Cathay*, is not the original—those who want it must take the trouble to get it in the original language, for it cannot otherwise be gotten at all—but the contemporary poem. "The Seafarer" is a great poem in Pound, as great as the original, different from it and—the important point—more important to the twentieth century than the original superb poem. The delicate line has shown its ability to take the full weight of all the reinforcing power of English, and still retain its pure singing quality:

> Bitter breast-cares have I abided,
> Known on my keel many a care's hold
> And dire sea-surge, and there I oft spent
> Narrow nightwatch nigh the ship's head
> While she tossed close to cliffs. Coldly afflicted
> My feet were by frost benumbed.

Compare this use of the alliterative technique with that of Swinburne on the one hand, and of Hopkins and Doughty on the other. This poem blends the three types of poetry mentioned above, and is a remarkable achievement. The bleak, almost harsh atmosphere is echoed by the Hellenistic "Doria," where the cold bare elemental feeling is achieved by means as pared-down as "The Seafarer" is reinforced; but the link between the classical and the old Teutonic worlds is established, and Pound inherits both.

Other, lesser poems continue the development of his increasingly superb technical resources; and there is no such thing as "technique" without "matter," the thing made without the thing said. In their different ways the "Dieu qui l'a faicte" paraphrase, "The Return," "Ortus," "Salutation," "Causa," all consolidate the gains, now melody uppermost, now image, now "the dance of intellect." An interesting poem is "Dance Figure," which reads like a missing poem from the poet of the Song of Solomon. This aspect of Pound's work has been commented on little, if at all. The tradition he "drew from the air" includes, and includes as few poets have ever been able to include it in English, the great Hebrew strand—quite as much as the Roman, the Greek or the Teutonic. This is too obvious to need laboring: let the reader compare this poem with the early "Night Litany," and then keep his mind alert for the appearance of this note in Pound's work, and the point is made. He is, indeed, a psalmist first, and anything else after; not so much a prophet as a psalmist who has wandered into the wrong century.

The poem to Whitman in this group reminds us that Whitman too was essentially a psalmist, that the American experience is somehow calling for that kind of poetry. Yet the Whitman poem is less than convincing. Whitman was no "father," so little "pig-headed" that he is almost tolerance and acquiescence themselves: the broken wood that Pound is carving is not new, not broken by Whitman, but as old as Homer and as European as Browning. Pound, moreover, is doing quite a bit of wood-chopping himself. But what other twentieth-century poet can speak with the

Opening page of Pound's typescript of a small unpublished book, The Music of Beowulf, circa *late 1920's*.

THE MUSIC OF BEOWULF

The rest of the audience heard either a sequence of uncomprehended gaelic or the clumsy words of an unsatisfactory translation. Philologists do not in any great multitude flock to Aeolian Hall (Bond St. in the City of London.)

I was there to pay my ~~weekly~~ rent, to amuse myself, to increase my mental holdings. In a London dead from the neck up the three or four possible concerts a fortnight a fortnight were the only phenomena a man could inspect with any cerebral interest ; and in an england scared out of its nether garment by the terror of anything likely to cause thought in any form, mild, milder or mildest, music was the only last and only ~~s~~ remaining subject that any ~~s~~ editor (the one last and only remaining editor) thought it safe to allow me to turn loose on.

Snivveling war profite~~urs~~, abject lackeys etc, disliked " colloquial language " ; any form of mental correlation', the " perception of relations" ~~~~~~~~~~~~~~~~~~~~~~~~ which Aristotle long since noted as symptomatic of metal life were not at that season in favour. The sottialer was ~~s~~ filled to overflowing ; if I am to recall the London of that dreary day , I shd. also recall the fattening editor of a ~~XXXX~~ by-a-new-title-owned and ~~XXXX~~ even-today-extant weekly telling me that the word "aphrodisiac" should never appear in print . I confess that I had mentioned the ballet. However the

A version of "Canto XLV," "With Usura," in the poet's own hand.

tones of the Authorized Version? Genuinely, sib with it? And here again the apparent "archaism" has the same character: it purifies and cleanses the instrument. His point of contact with his originals is "purity" of mind, almost of piety in the presence of the Real.

In the poem called "The Rest" he endorses Joyce's injunction: "exile" as a means of surviving unbroken the hostility of one's countrymen to their living creators; but not the additional "silence and cunning." No writer can be "silent": if he could, there would be no trouble, he would be dead and safe. The poem, though, strikes a new note of contemporaneity, of vivid speech which is still poetry:

> You of the finer sense
> Broken against false knowledge,
> You who can know at first hand,
> Hated, shut in, mistrusted;

this is as up to date as tomorrow's newspaper, but the writing is made to last. "Dum Capitolium Scandet" says no more than is true, and says it incomparably; now we are getting immediate utterance in poem after poem, now that the tools have been sharpened, the broken wood roughed out. In "To Kalon" he says in sixteen words what is every honest poet's experience of the Muse:

> Even in my dreams you have denied yourself to me
> And sent me only your handmaids.

This immediacy of utterance is the result of a labor at technique which is unique in our time.

In the *Cathay* volume we get a poetry quite unique in English. This is pure achievement, not a developing of some half-forgotten tradition, but invention in the true sense, as Eliot saw. Here the three aspects of poetry blend together to create a fully mature poetry which has no forebears in the language. It is a poetry of incomparable lightness and deftness of touch, sweetness of melody, crisp with the crispness of the best prose (cf. "River-Merchant's Wife" with certain aspects of Jane Austen's work). The imagery plays in and out quietly, unobtrusively, subdued to the human as natural sensations in life are. "Exile's Letter" is a superb English poem. What we owe to the original poet we cannot know, but what we owe to Pound is obvious to all but those who will not see. This is the highest peak of English verse in this century up to the time of its appearance. This he must have known as the poem took shape under his pen, and I envy him the joy of that realization; it is the only real reward a poet can have, it is a rare one even in the best, and many good workers never know it at all: that ultimate satisfaction, of incomparable yet humble well-being, balance, rest, which is all too fleeting. From there on, stroke after stroke breaks through, the rock splits, he comes at the Hesperides. The English language, long fallow, seemingly worn out, has borne again, and those of us who look on at this common miracle know that we must not call a language "dead" till we have the strength to bury it. We Scots have had this experience this century, seen the desert blossom, the darkness sing. Norway has seen it, Provence has seen it, Greece has seen it, Israel is seeing it, Ireland—count not your corpses before they are dead. But if English cannot be suspected of having worn itself out as a medium of the creative imagination, it is surely a significant thing that in this century a disproportionate amount of what has been achieved in it has been done by Americans, Irishmen, Welshmen and Scots. English has fallen to a lower level in England itself since Pound and Eliot infused new life into it than the level they found it at: the Georgian poets were at least poets, not anti-poets. But I digress. *Cathay* is a great achievement, and unique: "What is the use of talking / and there is no end of talking / There is no end of things in the heart": and no end of words for the things, if a man of gift and dedication comes to sing them.

With the *Lustra* of 1915 enters a new assurance, a new strength, a greater imaginative power; the language, the verse has been hammered out, the discipline which liberates these things. Eliot has praised "Near Perigord," and I have little to add to that; it has met with due praise. I might even take a little away, by saying that I am least at ease with Pound when he is most familiar with Browning. No man can take liberties with Browning; he stands alone, and to invite comparison with him is to invite eclipse by him in the realm of psychological characterization in which he is supreme. Pound is as good a poet as Browning; I think he is a better—on his own ground, not on Browning's. Yet "Perigord" is a triumph of that ease and freedom of controlled movement, of exact cadence, which is Pound's especial glory. I don't like the famous last line, "A broken bundle of mirrors . . . !" It is a "conceit" in the bad sense, a little bit cheap; I suspect that they were gey tinkerish trashy mirrors. "To A Friend Writing on Cabaret Dancers," on the other hand, seems to me to be a poem that has had less attention than it deserves, and only Pound could have written it; it is full of a confident identity entirely his own, and the little sketch of Pepita is sharp and clear, with a fineness of edge not to be found in Browning, nor anyone else in English. The paraphrases of Provençal poems in "Langue d'Oc" is the technical perfectionist at his exercises again, but what exercises they are—vocalizes by Caruso. The *vers de société* of "Moeurs Contemporains" is of course a preparation for *Mauberley*. I must confess here that, much as I admire the technical mastery they display, I am uneasy with them. They represent a superficial aspect of Pound, a sophistication and cleverness which is assumed rather than native; the real Pound is not superficial. There is something distasteful to me in this fashionable taking-off of fashionableness; it's Henry Jamesy, and that means it's not Ezra Pound. The man who wrote *Cathay* was already ticking far beyond this level of urbane poetic dandyism. They are unconvincng (so to me is "Portrait d'une Femme," an early poem, and for the same reasons), brittle as chipped enamel; they embarrass me with a kind of insincerity. They are only two-dimensional, somehow, thin; Eliot could have done them better, adding a third dimension. But Eliot could not have written *Cathay*, nor any of the poems praised above.

The *Homage to Sextus Propertius* has been much attacked and much praised (by Professor Kenner most intelligently). This mixture of paraphrase and parody seems to me to be a superb poem in its own right, once one has cleared out of the way the idiotic notion that Pound is "translating"; then it doesn't matter tuppence even if he does (and he does) render *conticuere omens* as "They were all County Kerry men," or *stant litore puppes* as "There stands a litter of puppies." Anybody who looks at the poem through solemn academic spectacles after reading that little lot, as he checks up on how "good" Mr. Pound's "translation" is, deserves to be bottomized for life. What happens here is that Pound brings off in verse the kind of high-comic re-creation of Roman character that Graves does so superbly in his Claudius books:

> Could you endure such promiscuity?
>   She was not renowned for fidelity;
> But to jab a knife in my vitals, to have passed on
>   a swig of poison,
> Preferable, my dear boy, my dear Lynceus,
> Comrade, comrade of my life, of my purse, of my
>   person;
> But in one bed, in one bed alone, my dear Lynceus,
>   I deprecate your attendance;
> I would ask a like boon of Jove.

That is superb in its light, deft, pernickety humor, and it is once again—and again this is the point—unique in English. Freedom within the law, elegance, grace, delicacy, sophisticated humor, a new balance of wit, a new flexibility of the instrument and nuances of ironic tone. This is no place for the solemn "scrutiny"; we sit back and enjoy the rich fun. Pound has brought off another technical triumph.

The *Hugh Selwyn Mauberley* volume has been much praised and perhaps overpraised. Those who see in it a new crystallization, the summit achievement of all the long years of laborious apprenticeship, certainly are that much in the right; but to go on to praise this poem sequence at the expense of the Cantos is sheer nonsense. It is a sort of Good-bye to All That, Pound's farewell to England, to the obstinate isles where money matters more than value, and value matters more than worth. The first poem is superb: "Pour l'élection de son sepulchre." Here indeed is the kind of fusion of technique and experience Eliot speaks so well of in his introduction to the *Selected Poems.* Yet, as in all his *vers de société,* I have my reservations, my slightly itchy uncomfortableness in their presence: they are not the best Pound; they are a Pound who is going, a *persona* he is sloughing off, a cast skin, and I for one am glad to see it go. "There's more enterprise in walking naked." His true Penelope was Flaubert; all right, but Flaubert had an eye like a searchlight. When he turned it on the object, the thing stood out as if it were radioactive. *Mauberley* talks too much and sees too little—lacks just that "focus" of vision which is so markedly a quality of Flaubert. It is, in a sense, two-dimensional, thin, spread out rather than rounded, despite the unprecedented condensation, for I speak here not of its mental content but of its sensual "world." The phanopoeia is thin, the logopoeia a bit too usurping. Yet there is here, in the fifth section of this first poem, a piece whch stands outside all mere critical carping. This is not just *an* elegy for the dead of World War I, it is *the* elegy:

> There died a myriad,
> And of the best, among them,
> For an old bitch gone in the teeth,
> For a botched civilization,
>
> Charm, smiling at the good mouth,
> Quick eyes gone under earth's lid,
>
> For two gross of broken statues,
> For a few thousand battered books.

Here is the true elegiac note, stark, classical, that brings the pinprick to the eye—Say to the Lakedemonioi that we lie here. . . . Pound was not one of those who "went to it," but it is fitting that it should be he, the suffering onlooker as his friends went down one by one, who writes the last heart-stounding word on that great lost generation (I write out of one even more lost, for we had no illusions to lose) of soldier-creators; not only the Owens, Rosenbergs, Hulmes who died, but those who came back, Graves, Sassoon, Read, wounded in the mind by an experience even their strength and fineness found impossible to digest. Those two central lines speak a wealth of personal suffering in this most impersonal of poets, the pity and grief are devastating in their stark simplicity. And it is not that the "best" were in fact dying for the old bitch, the statues and the books, but "believing in old men's lies." And those who came back, came back to what? To "usury age-old and age-thick and liars in public places," to grow up sons for the next holocaustal throes of a dying and evil social system, the one in which my own generation was caught up and decimated, adding to Pound's roll call of the missing the names of Keyes, Douglas, Lewis and many others, and most tragic of all, those who had not yet announced their names. Let all accusers, denigrators, defamers of character, let all those who urge legitimate complaints, set this down: it was Pound who wrote their epitaph, in pity, outrage and pain. "Canto XLV" grew out of that pity, outrage and pain, as did so much of his subsequent life.

In the title poem itself, and in "The Age Demanded," he writes his own epitaph, with equal simplicity, but with none of the accompanying pity:

> Non-esteem of self-styled 'his betters'
> Leading, as he well knew,
> To his final
> Exclusion from the world of letters.

So much the worse for the "world of letters."

I have exhausted my space in getting to the beginning. No matter, the Cantos are not in any hurry, they are not going anywhere, Mont Blanc is not a whore passing in the street. Of Pound's criticism it must be said that one goes to it for direction, not for evaluation; it is equipment to take on the journey, not a hotel at the end of it. No such equipment can be got anywhere else, and the young poet who is without it is an optimistic ass. The academic who thinks he is above it is an obstruction to the young in his charge, failing to give true direction, and probably also giving false. Dr. Leavis notwithstanding, the non-practicing critic is rarely of any consequence, and most often an obstruction; it is to practitioners themselves that the criticism of their craft ultimately belongs. And Pound is the maximal practitioner of our time. One cannot ignore any part of his work, and this is particularly true of what the obscurantists like to call "his monetary theories." Here, of course, Pound has done no more than tell the simple obvious truth that the Western world is the victim of the most colossal fraud by private financiers that has been perpetrated in all human history. It is for telling this truth, of course, that he has barely escaped with his life. I disagree with much of his detail in his vision of finance-capitalist society, but not with his general view, and I applaud his caring about such things. Whatever "side" one is on in the present showdown, Pound has made it possible for poets to write about history and the things that really matter socially, and impossible to confine themselves ever again to moonshine and mountain daisies. Morality is a matter of economic behavior, and the poet's concern with human values begins with money and worth, though it may end in New Jerusalem. Pound is unhappy to wake up to find himself on the side that made Belsen; but I am unhappy to have been on the side that made Dresden and Hiroshima and Nagasaki. Let us forgive the past and get on with the job.

Old maestro of the incomparable cadence, it's no poor achievement for your first eighty years.

Title page of Pound's Digest of the Analects, *Milan, 1937.*

CONFUCIUS

DIGEST
OF THE
ANALECTS

MILAN
XV

Colophon, Digest of the Analects.

"all'Insegna del Pesce d'Oro"

Di questo volumetto nella versione di Ezra Pound, a cura di Giovanni Scheiwiller si sono stampati dalle Industrie Grafiche Pietro Vera di Milano il 15 - 6 - 1937 - XV, 220 esemplari numerati su carta uso mano e 25 esemplari su carta "Japon" numerati da I a XXV per gli amici del libro

ESEMPLARE N. 127

THE ROCK DRILL[1]

by Wyndham Lewis

THE LETTERS OF EZRA POUND are a pedagogic volcano. One of the finest poets of his time, his gift was indissolubly linked with the function of prophet and teacher. He could not create without at the same time teaching and he could not teach except as a product of creation. (He writes: "It's all rubbish to pretend that art isn't didactic. A revelation is always didactic.") He is a double-barreled genius of simultaneous action. But whereas his teaching is volcanic, his creation is a highly disciplined discharge.

As literary history these *Letters* are of first-class importance. You see him hammering away, in letter after letter, at the reluctant Harriet Monroe, editor of the American magazine *Poetry*. This was mainly during the years of World War I. It was his object to purge, as far as lay in his power, this important "little magazine" of what was second-rate and parochial. His rock-drill action is impressive: he blasts away tirelessly, prodding and coaxing its mulish editress. His action, of course, was not confined to *Poetry*. He directed a fire from his strategic position in London upon all the archaistic *slush,* as he called it, produced by the song-birds of his native land. I do not say that it was single-handed that

[1] A review for the *New Statesman,* April 7, 1951, of *The Letters of Ezra Pound,* ed. by D. D. Paige (London: Faber & Faber, Ltd., 1951).

he effected a prosodic purgation, but he certainly contributed very largely to an up-to-date standard of verse-writing in that country.

The main character of this renaissance (the term he would use in writing to John Quinn) was an evolution from soft to hard. "Imagism stands," he writes, "for hard light, clear edges." And Imagism was the official name of his doctrine. In a letter to Harriet Monroe he catalogues what is needed as follows:

> Poetry must be *as well written as prose* . . . departing in no way from speech save by a heightened intensity. There must be no book words, no periphrases, no inversions. It must be as simple as de Maupassant's best prose, and as hard as Stendhal's . . . . Rhythm must have meaning. It can't be merely a careless dash off, with no grip and no real hold to the words and sense, a tumpy tum tumty tum tum ta. There must be no clichés, set phrases, stereotyped journalese. The only escape from such is by precision . . . . Objectivity and again objectivity . . . no hindside-beforeness, no straddled adjectiveness (as "addled mosses dank"), no Tennysonianness of speech; nothing—nothing that you couldn't in some circumstances, in the stress of some emotion, actually say.

Elsewhere he speaks of the "hardness bred by reading Dante, or . . . Aquinas." Add this indication of the source of his own hardness, at all events, and with the above catalogue you have the core of his teaching. How today's great novelty is tomorrow's commonplace! For every injunction you have just read was extremely necessary at the time it was written, but today they represent a *since qua˙ non* of every writer's equipment, although naturally the disciplines imposed, more especially the *hardness* enjoined by Pound and others, have been rejected by many. People always tend to sink back into the "slush" from which they are periodically dragged with so much difficulty.

Dante we have seen him indicate as a teacher of the "hard edge," of precision. But nineteenth-century French poetry, and indeed the whole of French poetry from the seventeenth century onward, was possibly a greater influence than any other for Pound and Eliot in his earlier verses. In his defense, when attacked as leader of the international school by Williams on behalf of the *echt Americanisch* school, Pound writes: "I sent over French models, which have given six hundred people a means of telling something nearer the truth than they would have done senza." Note *French* models. Théophile Gautier, Tristan Corbière, Jules Laforgue are masters of concise statement, of the natural in contrast with the poetic, and some knowledge of them and other French *petit-maîtres* is necessary for an understanding of how French techniques and intellection were substituted, both in the U.S. and in England, for nineteenth-century English romanticism. In the case of Mr. Eliot, his critical writings switched the contemporary English mind back from the early nineteenth century to the seventeenth and eighteenth, from the emotional romantic lyricism of Shelley and Keats to the "harder" rational texture of such as Dryden and Crabbe.

The enormous influence, to my mind for the good, exerted by Ezra Pound can be most clearly seen in his effect upon Mr. Eliot, and also upon W. B. Yeats. The extent to which Pound influenced the former is generally recognized; but the fact that Yeats's last period would probably never have occurred without Ezra Pound's promptings is, I think, not understood, and these *Letters* should be very suggestive in that connection.

The tone of the *Letters* almost from the beginning is authoritative, not to say pontificatory. It is a rather strange tone for the author of *Cathay,* some might think. But if we remember that the voice of the Bull Moose president resounded in his ears in his young days, it is perhaps less to be wondered at that Ezra himself should have wished to wield the "Big Stick"; that we should hear him saying, "I cannot be expected to keep up sufficient interest in the state of public imbecility to go on being 'astringent' perpetually." So Ezra when he put on the prophet's robe borrowed the voice of the Bull Moose; but it echoes playfully in these letters, and it is, I believe, a fact that he never lost his temper, at least not publicly. Amy Lowell, it is true, did succeed in shaking the ivory tower once or twice, especially when she persisted in employing the term Imagiste, whereas Vers Libre was the appropriate word in her case. But although the tower shook, Ezra was still laughing at the top of it. Really one of his major assets has been this equanimity; he has not read his Chinese philosophers for nothing.

This book can be of no interest to anyone but a writer. It is a craftsman speaking throughout about his craft, and the single-minded concentration is magnificent. They are the shoppiest letters it is possible to imagine, unless Cézanne had been a very intelligent and literate painter, when we might have had something of the same sort. There is probably no finer translator in the English language, and the dozen or so pages of his notes on Binyon's translation of the "Purgatorio" is of great interest. An eventual edition of all his letters should be one of the finest craft books that we have.

After World War I Ezra Pound left England, cursing; he apparently attempted to settle in Paris, but he did not seem to get on there, although he learned to play the bassoon. In February, 1925, he settled in Rapallo; there he lived until American soliders took him away to Genoa in 1944. The letters of the Rapallo period are, in isolation, even finer than those of the English period, but at Rapallo he was not building a "renaissance"; that had been built. The *Letters* are full of elaborations of earlier statements; they have not the dramatic *élan* of the pioneer hacking his way through the bush. Usury lifts its ugly head: economics, not heard of before, becomes a major interest.

This greatest living American exile apparently did not realize that politics was a different dimension from literature, and now they have him boxed up in the nation's capital, *echt Americanisch* by habitat perforce; he will hardly regain his freedom, once more to sing and scold by the Latin Sea, alas!

From Pound's corrected typescript of "Vou Club," an article on a group of Japanese poets. Although written for the Milwaukee Globe, *it was published in Ronald Duncan's* Townsman, *January, 1938. (Humanities Research Center, University of Texas.)*

I myself feel rather like a grizzly bear faced by a bunch of weasels. It is the Mongoose spring, the cameleon's tongue quickness. All the moss and fuzz that for 20 years we have been trying to scrape off our language, these young men start without it. They see the crystal set, the chemical laboratory and the pine tree with untrammeled clearness.

As to their being a or the most active new club of poets in Tokio, I doubt if any one city contains two such clubs. I knew that nowhere in Europe is there any such vertex of poetic alertness. Tokio takes over, where Paris stopped.

Make no mistake, the thought is not absent from these poems. The Japanese poet has gone from one peak of it to another faster than our slow wits permit us to follow before we have got used to his pace.

Ezra Pound

P/S/ not for print.
I think it wd. be enormous less to GLOBE not to take this opportunity to be FIRST in introducing the VOU/
Further notices can be left to literary magazines. But this IS news item.
If you don't SEE it, I shall be disappointed. In any case, please send SOON either proofs, or the mss/ for print or reprint in England. Where Globe is unlikely to be on sale.

Little Review made a record. I think in ten years time GLOBE ought to be able to " point with pride "

202

Pound's corrected typescript of "Brace of Axioms" and opening of "Musik, as Mistaught," both published in the July, 1938, Townsman. *(Humanities Research Center, University of Texas.)*

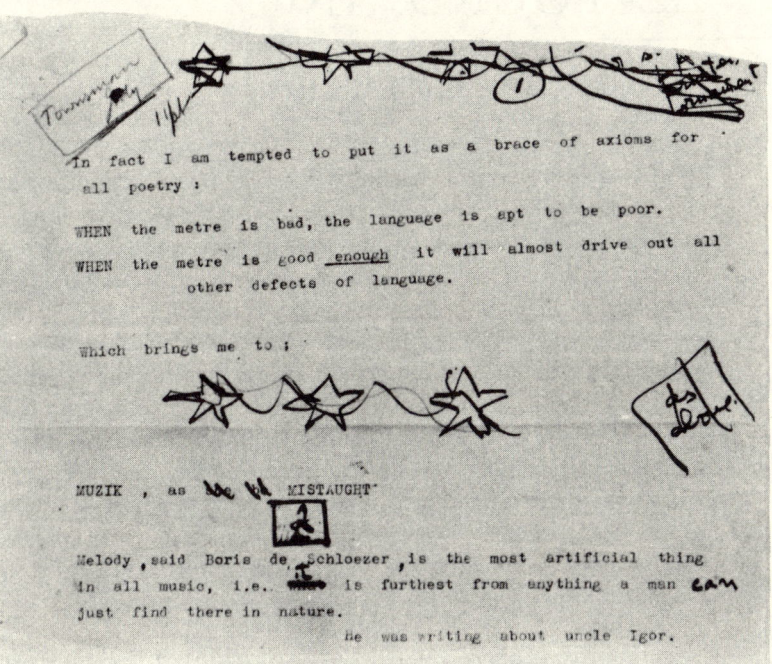

EZ POUND, INC.

by *Joseph Fetler Malof*

POUND'S ATTENTION has been on the shared experiences of the tribe. As a teacher he has served not so much to transmit anything as to increase the communal partaking of the important things. That is what his poems do also. Opening a page of his poetry (one of the Cantos, for example) is like entering into the half-light of a museum, sometimes curious and sometimes stunning with unexpected displays. The effect is indeterminate but not fuzzy; the objects are sharp and clear but do not combine into any smart patterns of significance. It is more exhibition than message, and the search for the meaning of the Cantos is not as much to the point as the awareness of how they are arranged and illuminated to be provocative. The citations and allusions do not make a repository of records but an exhibit of experiences.

Pound's reader must "learn" a poem just as he must learn a work of music—or, rather, he must continually be in the process of learning it, this being the experience the poem makes. It is not a matter of translation and footnotes but of experiencing relationships more clearly. Simple poems want to be learned as much as the documentary ones. Erudition is not the basis of the central activity, but Pound demands to be accurate in his own experiences. He does not require the reader to have mimicked his own program of studies; what he needs is a reader who can relish the experience of becoming cultured. So the knowledge may be esoteric but the tone is colloquial: knowledge is good for art only as experience, and what the reader learns from the poem is a part of his activity, not an acquisition. The "foreign stuff" may give depth, emphasis, richness, relevance, scope, but the essentials are already there. Leave blanks, says Pound, and go on. The reader gets as much as he is prepared for or cares to take: "If you have not the tongues, seek out the leisurely Chaucer." It is a museum of incipient, not reconstructed, experiences.

To inquire after the meanings of poems is to question the meaning of activity. More important is the awareness of production, blast and flow. Pound usually refers to "meaning" as one of the elements within the poem, like sound-movement; he speaks of the core in terms of "attention." The Cantos are a world of corporate experiences as arranged by Pound the director. The organization of these experiences into a major order may be there, but only as the product rather than as the production.

Pound's more obscure poetry is in danger of being enshrined for the wrong reasons. But riddle-solving and allusion-hunting have prompted many good analyses which lead, expectedly, to different interpretations. The poetry is charged to stimulate individual experiences. Specific meanings are secondary, however well they shape or illuminate the primary blast. Pound's kind of form makes for mental complexity but experiential simplicity, and in this sense his obscure poems are easier to read than those requiring the reader to follow an external argument.

Pound's objection to the academies has been on the basis of form as well as substance. The forms in the Cantos are universal and tribal, not historical residues, so the structure of the poem will not be seen adequately from any single level. The coherence to be had from thematic, narrative, tonal, historic, emotional, mythical and associative patterns does not make up a "major form" (to use Eliot's phrase) of art. Neither will the idea of "current form"—of the unpredictable moment only—complete the picture. With Pound's work especially, form must also be understood in terms of what it is not, where and how a boundary is laid out between all that which belongs to the work and all that which lies outside. One of the essential features of the Cantos, as Pound has said, is the lack of any total, overriding commitment to local forms, those that use history, argument, etc., as their binding-matter. Such forms are clearly there, but no local element in the Cantos is fixed permanently. Only beyond the outer boundary is there the realm of definitive consistency, fixity, stasis. So the formal obligation that Pound assumes is a commitment to diversity: he means to get at the flow of experience in a large way. To have diversity without arbitrariness he uses superimposition, juxtaposition, metamorphosis, repetition and other kinds of movements. The reader's object is not to pin the passing segments but to become involved with the general movement as well as he can at the time. The major organization of the movement will occur by itself, or will fail, but cannot be sought out intellectually. In terms of their major form, the Cantos operate like a work of music.

The action of the Cantos is universal in two ways. For Pound as the protagonist it comes as a spatial and temporal simultaneousness of experiences laced together with various kinds of local form. For the reader it creates experiences shared by the entire corporation of readers. There is a common interest: a conceptual awareness of fixity and a perceptual awareness of flux. One speaks of poetic language as creating a flow and movement, punctuated by specific features. But for Pound it is ordinary existence that flows. The words of a poem in a way arrest this normal movement and create movements of their own, making counterpoint or descant for the movements they imitate. Sculpture is the most stable way of arresting the flux, music the most fluid. Something like ideographic poetry, combining the two, can produce movement of the highest order: the fixity reconciled with the flux. What Pound always is driving at is major form, the harmonious movement of the permanent, the recurrent and the casual. For all the involutions of substance, the movement of the Cantos is as simple—or, rather, direct—as experience itself. There is no point in arranging to leave the world a beautiful heritage: no fixed meanings should be allowed to divert attention from the primary movement. That is Pound's legacy.

Wrapper of Orientamenti, Venice, 1944, one of the rarest of all Pound's books.

Pound's typescript of a section of the Pisan Cantos, *typed by the author at the U.S. detention camp at Pisa in 1945 and sent to his daughter, now Princess Mary de Rachewiltz.*

```
                                              ms 251
made courage or made order or made grace
   pull down thy vanity , pull down ,

Learn of the green world what can be thy place
In scaled invention or true artistry
Pull down thy vanity
                Paquin pull down !
   The green casque has outdone your elegance,

" Master thyself, then others shall thee beare "
   Pull down thy vanity
Thou art a beaten dog beneath the hail
A swolen magpie in a fitful sun
Half black half white
Nor knowst'ou wing from tail
Pull down thy vanity
                    How mean thy hates
Fostered in falsity
            pull down thy vanity
   Rathe to destroy, niggard in charity,
Pull down thy vanity
              I say pull down .

But to have done instead of not doing
            this is not vanity
To have ,with decency , knocked
That a Blunt should open .
      To have gathered from the air a live tradition
or from a fine old eye the unconquered flame
This is not vanity.
   Here error is all in the not done,
   all in the diffidence that faltered,

              ( CANTO )

Then with his hunting dog I see a cloud

" Guten Morgen , Mein Herr " yells the black boy from the
                                                jo-cart
( Jeffers , Lovell and Harley
      Also Mr Walls who has lent me a razor
      Persha , Nadasky and Harbell )

Swinburne my only miss
                and I didn't know
he had been to see Landor
            and  they told me this that and tother
and when old Mathews
   went, he saw the three teacups
      two for Watts Dunton who liked to let his tea cool,
So old Elkin had only one glory :
      He did carry Algernon's suit case once
When he , Elkin , first came to London,
But given what I know now I 'd have broken the door in
      or got thru it somehow ... Dirce's shade
              or a blackjack .
```

From Pound's corrected typescript of a two-page comment on Ezra Pound, *a book of essays edited by Peter Russell, 1950. (Humanities Research Center, University of Texas.)*

An Examen #1

"A very able presentation of present state of criticism in Britain

and an american might regret that the british critics seem to show up in so favorable a light when compared to the "american " ooJJJJsIriaIiIjJItaIIaaistates contributions, the two canadians having a better grip on the subject

especially if we deduct the two canadian writers who are as good as anything in the volume.

Of course if No Carranza government of Mexico just isn't interesting (vide Miss Sitwell's view) it is just too bad, and if poetry is to be reduced limited to prosody and blue china , a good deal of Homer , pig-styes, rafts and so on would have to go by the board. It is a little hard to find warrant for a static, as distinct from a renew society

as distinct from one in a state of constant renewal , in Dr Pound's writings. or perhaps

But perhaps one's greatest worry is the lack of contemporary awareness in so many of the distinguished contributors. The present critic , to tell the turth , can only feel " at year ", if we be permitted that expression , by analogy to " at home", with Mays Wykes-Joyce and Swabey. He is indeed moved to writing this paragraph only in the hope of bringing one or two sentences of these critics into what he believes to be more accurate accord with Dr Pound's hhh own view

of Ezra Pound, edited by P.R.

BBC THIRD PROGRAM

EZRA POUND
TRANSLATIONS FROM THE CHINESE

Selected and Introduced
by
Denis Goacher

Readers: Hugh Burden
         Denis Goacher
         Olive Gregg

TRANSMISSION:	Friday 24th May 1963 10.30-11.0 P.M.	Third
PRE-RECORD:	Monday 20th May 1963	5.0-6.0 P.M.
REHEARSE:	Monday 20th May 1963	2.15-5.0 P.M.

Denis Goacher

GOACHER:

For every reader of Pound's own poetry, there must be ten who have at least glanced at his versions from the Chinese. Two remarks, by T. S. Eliot and Ford Madox Ford respectively, have achieved almost proverbial status: Pound "is the inventor of Chinese poetry for our time"; *Cathay* "is the most beautiful book in the language." The translations fall into three distinct groups and only the first, *Cathay*, is well known; imagine the effect if, in 1915, one had come across this for the first time:

BURDEN:

> This boat is of shato-wood, and its gunwales
>   are cut magnolia,
> Musicians with jewelled flutes and with pipes
>   of gold
> Fill full the sides in rows, and our wine
> Is rich for a thousand cups.
> . . . .
> And I have moped in the Emperor's garden, awaiting
>   an order-to-write!
> I looked at the dragon-pond, with its willow-
>   coloured water
> Just reflecting the sky's tinge,
> And heard the five-score nightingales aimlessly
>   singing . . .

GOACHER:

For many of us this *tour de force* is the justification of a century of aestheticism: but it is also aestheticism completely renovated; it introduces potent, alien subject matter, and the language is clean and fresh; one feels a mighty dredging operation has been done. Moreover, there is genuinely new music, which is rare enough in all literatures (Mr. Eliot was to give a similar shock a couple of years later in *Prufrock*).

"And I have moped in the Emperor's garden, awaiting an order to write!" That cadence has been copied, elaborated, diluted a thousand times since.

The poem is by Rihaku, which is Sino-Japanese for Li T'ai Po, the great T'ang poet. Pound used the name because in making *Cathay* he was helped by the notes of two Japanese professors as well as by those of the American, Ernest Fenollosa.

One of the pleasures of *Cathay* is to watch Pound finding his own tone of voice—as in the last two lines of this "Sennin Poem by Kakuhaku":

Burden:

> The red and green kingfishers
>   flash between the orchids and clover,
>   One bird casts its gleam on another.
>
> Green vines hang through the high forest,
> They weave a whole roof to the mountain,
> The lone man sits with shut speech,
> He purrs and pats the clear strings.
> . . . .
> But you, you dam'd crowd of gnats,
> Can you even tell the age of a turtle?

Goacher:

Let us now skip nearly forty-five years from the first to the third group of Pound's translations. Long ago he announced his intention of doing the ancient collection of Chinese poetry, the Book of Odes, after he had finished the Cantos. In the early years of his incarceration, unable to continue with his own poem, he set to work on the Shih King (or Shih Ching). This anthology of 305 pieces was long thought to have been selected by Confucius, a theory now generally rejected, though it seems certain that he was their musical editor. When the *Classic Anthology* first appeared in 1954, I asked Pound how he thought it compared with his other translations. He replied, "Quite different! There's nothing of me in 'em—except technique," and when I pointed out that it would inevitably be compared with *Cathay* he said, "Rihaku is obviously a different dish from the *Odes*. Anyway, you can compare the first in *Cathay* with the present version, 167. In general, the technique of translating Chinese poetry had not advanced from *Cathay*—at least, so far as I know."

Here, then, is the "Song of the Bowmen of Shu" as it first appeared in *Cathay*.

BURDEN:

> Here we are, picking the first fern-shoots
>   And saying: When shall we get back to
>   our country?
> Here we are because we have the Ken-nin for
>   our foemen,
> We have no comfort because of these Mongols.
> We grub the soft fern-shoots,
> When anyone says "Return", the others are
>   full of sorrow . . . .

GOACHER:

And this is how Pound renders it in the *Classic Anthology*:

> Pick a fern, pick a fern, ferns are high
> "Home", I'll say: home, the year's gone by,
> no house, no roof, these huns on the hoof.
> Work, work, work, that's how it runs,
> We are here because of these huns . . . .

We see that a complete effort has been made to overcome chinoiserie—even the chinoiserie of Pound's own making. Someone, I think Hugh Kenner, said that this collection could be taken as a handbook of English verse procedures; "procedures" is a pretty stuffy word, but there certainly is a great variety of form—folk songs, ballads, dramatic narrative, measured odes—above all, songs:

> "Hid! Hid!" the fish-hawk saith,
> by isle in Ho the fish-hawk saith:
>   "Dark and clear,
>   Dark and clear,
> So shall be the prince's fere."
>   . . . .

> High reed caught in ts'ai grass
> > so deep her secrecy;
> lute sound in lute sound is caught,
> > touching, passing, left and right.
> Bang the gong of her delight.

Here is another from the first, folk song, section:

BURDEN:

> In fleecy coats with five white tassels,
> affable snakes, the great duke's vassals glide
> from his hall
> to tuck their court rations inside . . . .

GOACHER:

Now, two songs for a woman's voice which display Pound's wonderful kinetic knack:

GREGG:

> Lies a dead deer on yonder plain
> whom white grass covers,
> A melancholy maid in spring
> > is luck
> > for
> > lovers . . . .

GOACHER:

"The Pedlar."

GREGG:

> "Hill-billy, hill-billy come to buy
> silk in our market, apparently?
> toting an armful of calico.
> Hill-billy, hill-billy, not at all
> but come hither to plot my fall, . . .
> . . . .
> "Grow old with you," whom old you spite,
> K'i has its banks and every swamp an edge.
> Happy in pig-tails, laughed to hear your pledge,
> sun up, sun up, believing all you said,
> who in your acts reverse

> (as a matter of course)
> all that you ever said
> and for the worse,
> an end."

GOACHER:

No. 57, Pound calls an Epithalamium:

BURDEN:

> Tall girl with a profile,
> broidery neath a simple dress,
> brought from Ts'i her loveliness
> to Wei's marquisat.
> Younger sister of Tung-Kung
> ("Palace of the East", crown-prince)
> One sister of hers is the darling
> of the great lord of Hing,
> the other's man, T'an's viscount is . . . .

GOACHER:

No. 26 has a special poignance if we remember that this book was written during Ezra Pound's incarceration:

> Pine boat a-shift
> on drift of tide,
> for flame in the ear, sleep riven,
> driven; rift of the heart in dark
> no wine will clear,
> nor have I will to playe.
> . . . .
> . . . sorrow about the heart like an unwashed shirt, I
> clutch here at words,
> having no force to fly.

Among the "Elegantiae" or smaller Odes is a poem dating from approximately 770 B.C. which has an amusing topicality for us:

BURDEN:

> Heaven's worry, scurries to earth:
> twisty planning, what's to block it?

At sight of a good plan, they turn to rotten again,
the sight of their planning
gives me a pain.

First say yes, then say no;
good plan, no go,
but a rotten they dress in flummery,
the sight of their planning worries me.

> State
> all a wobble,
> scanners and boobs—
> a few left to gobble—
> bright boys and planners,
> some who'll "take trouble"
> all of a bubble
> down into quick-sand . . . .

GOACHER:

It is obvious that many of the Odes, indeed the majority, have a strong moral tone, very different from the hedonistic fatalism of the T'ang poets. Pound thinks of himself as a Confucian and has translated three of the Classics, but they are hardly suitable for this program: ethics seen through the medium of a poem are one thing, but shaped by prose (that battle axe Pound calls his prose, said Ford Madox Ford), they become very much more tendentious.

Here is No. 220, a "drinking" song:

BURDEN:

> And as at every drinking bout
> some can hold it and some pass out,
> we appoint, at every rally,
> a toast-master and his keep-tally
> so that those who can't hold their liquor
> or, as we say, run true to form,
> are kept from worse enormity
> of word or of activity;
> after three cups cannot tell lamb
> from horned ram, but still
> want more liquor ardently.

Denis Goacher

GOACHER:

A curiosity is one of the Songs of Cheng; Pound notes that Confucius said, "Banish the songs of Cheng," adding that he, Kung, seems to have regarded the tunes to these verses as a species of crooning or boogie-woogie.

> Hep-Cat Chung, don't jump my wall
> nor strip my mulberry boughs,
> The boughs don't matter
> But my brothers' clatter!
>   Have a heart, Chung,
>   it's awful . . . .

No. 55 carries the epigraph, "The bamboos grow well under good rule."

GREGG:

> Dry in the sun by corner of K'i
> green bamboo, bole over bole:
> Such subtle prince is ours
> to grind and file his powers
> as jade is ground by wheel;
> he careth his people's weal,
> stern in attent,
> steady as sun's turn bent
> on his folk's batterment
>   nor will he fail . . . .

GOACHER:

That is very fine, but the prevailing moral tone seems to make the Odes antipathetic to many of us; if we compare it immediately with "Poem by the Bridge at Ten-Shin," we can see why *Cathay* is so very much more popular:

> March has come to the bridge head,
> Peach boughs and apricot boughs hang
>   over a thousand gates,
> At morning there are flowers to cut the heart,
> And evening drives them on the eastward-flowing
>   waters . . . .

So when you hear someone saying that he doesn't like what Pound has produced since he really started to *learn* Chinese, you can have more than a suspicion that he's really objecting to what he thinks is the *content* of the Odes—as compared with *Cathay*. If so he has missed, for instance, No. 229:

GREGG:

>White the marsh flower that white grass
>>bindeth, my love's afar,
>I am alone.

>>2.
>White cloud and white dew shun,
>amid all flowers, none.
>Steep are the steps of heaven
>>to him unknown.

GOACHER:

It is weird to think that nowadays only an idealistic Communist, perhaps, can respond to this poem, which Pound calls "Fraternitas":

BURDEN:

>>Splendour recurrent
>>in cherry-wood
>>in all the world there is
>>nothing like brotherhood.

>>Brothers meet
>>in death and sorrow;
>>broken line, battle heat,
>>Brothers stand by;

>>In a pinch they collaborate
>>as the ling bird's vertebrae
>>when friends of either
>>protractedly just sigh . . . .

GOACHER:

For myself, I'm prepared to accept almost any didacticism if expressed as in No. 291, with which we end:

Speed, speed the plow
on south slopes now
grain is to sow
                       lively within.

. . . .

At harvest home kill a yellow bull,
by his curved horn is luck in full
(be he black-nosed seven foot high,
so tall's felicity.)

Thus did
men of old
who left us this land
to have and to hold.